Leonardo B. Dal Maso

ROME
OF THE CAESARS

Bonechi-Edizioni «Il Turismo»
Via dei Rustici, 5 - 50122 FIRENZE

COINS OF THE ROMAN EMPIRE

C.I. CAESAR
100 b.C. - 44 b.C.

AUGUSTUS
27 b.C. - 14 A.D.

TIBERIUS
14-37 A.D.

AGRIPPINA
14 b.C. - 37 A.D.

CALIGULA
37-41 A.D.

CLAUDIUS
41-54 A.D.

NERO
54-68 A.D.

GALBA
68-69 A.D.

VESPASIANUS
69-79 A.D.

TITUS
79-81 A.D.

DOMITIANUS
81-96 A.D.

NERVA 96-98 A.D.	**TRAIANUS-PLOTINA** 98-117 A.D.	**HADRIANUS** 117-138 A.D.
ANTONINUS PIUS 138-161 A.D.	**FAUSTINA** 138-160 A.D.	**M. AURELIUS** 161-180 A.D.
COMMODUS 180-192 A.D.	**IULIA DOMNA** 193-212 A.D.	**DIOCLETIANUS** 284-305 A.D.
MAXENTIUS 306-312 A.D.	**CONSTANTINUS** 312-337 A.D.	**CONSTANTINUS** (Versus)

FOREWORD

Any attempt to reconstruct the Rome of the Caesars, to imagine how its great historical events took place and what its private and public life were like, is an arduous and fascinating undertaking, in a city which endured and was constantly renewed for more than fourteen centuries, despite wars and natural disasters, fires and works of reconstruction, enlargements and the disfigurements wrought by the hand of man. It is an undertaking which involves a painstaking process of mental integration, a process which, if one wishes to avoid escaping into pure fantasy, can only be based on the archeological ruins still in existence and on the evidence which has come down to us from the ancient writers: but in both cases with all the limitations and reserves imposed by the fact that only a small part of either has reached us intact. Such a work of reconstruction, moreover, already fragmentary and full of gaps in itself, is rendered more difficult by the need to select, almost to extract, the scattered and corroded remains of the ancient city from among the living monuments and urban context of the papal and modern city, superimposed on the ancient one.

This is why the tourist fascinated by the ancient world, from Petrarch to Goethe and from Byron to Gogol and Stendhal, has always needed months, even years, to penetrate and assimilate the mystery of ancient Rome, why a long stay in the city was considered a basic necessity in the Humanist culture.

Today, however, although archeological discoveries and the restoriation of monuments has greatly increased the amount of evidence of the ancient world available to the visitor, long stays in the city have become extremely rare, due to the dynamic quality of modern life and the incessant haste with which it is pervaded. Long stays are indeed impossible with so-called mass tourism, which every year brings to Rome an increasingly large crowd of travellers, hungry for knowledge but restricted to brief, very limited itineraries, concentrated into visits of a few hours only. For them, the satisfaction of their cultural interests and their very understanding of the ancient world and of works of art depend almost entirely on the competence and expertise of the tourist guides.

Outstanding among these guides, Leonardo Dal Maso has taken advantage in thi book of twenty years' experience to offer visitors to Rome an amplified and integrated adjunct to the explanation, unavoidably summary, given vocally by the guide. It is an amplification which includes above all the placing of the monuments within a historical framework, giving a vision of the development of Rome's town-planning which allows the growth of the ancient city to be reconstructed, firstly through a wideranging historical summary, then through the description of the main monumental complexes (Palatine, Forum, Campidoglio, Imperial Fora). Furthermore, various monuments are grouped according to their type, so that appropriate comparisons can more easily be made (theatres, circuses, baths, triumphal arches). And finally a detailed description is given of some of the most illustrious monuments, such as the Colosseum, the Pantheon and the Ara Pacis. All this is accompanied by indispensable historical and artistic facts, which are enlivened, as if in a conversation, by information, episodes and curiosities drawn from the writings of the ancients, alternated with historical outlines of subjects of a more general nature, such as Rome's religion and its temples, its roads and communications, its work and workers.

Dal Maso's volume is thus not meant to be a severe systematic treatment or an arid listing of dates and technical descriptions, nor to obey, with the methodical rigidity of a guide with itineraries, the topographical or the historical-chronological criteria. Rather it is planned to include the basic elements of both, so as to allow the reader and visitor to Rome the possibility of capturing, so far as is possible within a human dimension, the spirit of the ancient world through its monuments, providing him as well with suggestions for a further deepening of his knowledge.

Among these suggestions is the brief excursion in the Capitoline Museums, inviting the reader to make the acquaintance of the treasures of classical figurative art contained in these and the other museums of the city, the Vatican, Villa Giulia, the Museo delle Terme, the Museo Barracco, the Antiquaria of the Forum, the Palatine, Hadrian's Villa and Ostia, to which a further booklet needs to be dedicated in order to give a worthy frame to the picture of ancient life.

Two more opportune enlargements are made to this picture in the general outlines of the two great monumental centres of Ostia and Hadrian's Villa which, although they were outside the walls of the city itself, were an integral part of ancient Rome: Ostia, the satellite city, as far as its commerce, provisioning, port activity and collective building programmes were concerned; Hadrian's Villa as the last site of the Imperial dwellings the outstanding creation of an architect-emperor who aspired to build the "ideal city".

Dal Maso, dealing with a wide variety of themes and points of view and assisted by the skilful selection of iconographical material, especially in the parallel reconstruction both of the monumental zones and of the individual works of architecture, fully achieves his aim of providing a conscientious tourist publication, which meets the desire for sufficient historical and artistic information and also satisfies various curiosities about the life and customs of the ancients.

Finally, a mention of the first Romano-Christian monuments serves as a prelude to the visit to that new Rome which was to carry on the function of the Eternal City in the history of civilisation, the Rome of the Popes, which will be the subject of a second volume. The vision of the Pantheon, symbol and as it were synthesis of the two Romes, brings this volume to a worthy close, after an ample analytic index, which alongside its role as an aid to the tourist's visit adds to the work's value as a useful and practical instrument of consultation.

Roberto Vighi
(Superintendent of Antiquities)

URBAN DEVELOPMENT OF ROME

Rome was founded, according to the ancient legend confirmed by archeological discoveries, in 753 B.C., and its first inhabitants were Latin shepherds who came from the Albani Hills. They settled in a small area on the left bank of the Tiver, at the place where it was easiest to cross the river because of the Tiberine Island, on what was later to be the site of the Boarian Forum (now Bocca della Verità), dominated by the Palatine Hill. On the top of the hill, in the strongest strategic position, the legendary founder, who took the name of Romulus, built the first circle of city walls, square in form. Soon the Latins on the Palatine were joined by the Sabines, who settled on the Quirinal Hill, and the small valley between the two hills became their meeting-place and market-place: the Forum.

During the first period of rule by kings (753-510 B.C.), two Latin kings and two Sabine kings alternated on the throne. Later the city was conquered by the Etruscans, a powerful people who made their appearance on the right bank of the Tiber and who dominated Rome under its last three kings, Servius Tullius and the two Tarquins. In these 243 years, the city spread to the other nearby hills, the Capitoline, Esquiline, Viminal, Coelian and Aventine, which together with the Palatine and the Quirinal constituted the Rome of the " Seven Hills ".

When the Latin population shook off this foreign domination in 510 B.C., the Republic was proclaimed. But in 390 B.C. the laborious expansion of the young state was interrupted by the invasion of the Gauls, led by Brennus, who devastated and set fire to the city before being repulsed by Camillus. " Hic manebimus optime " (" We shall do best to remain here "), said the senators after the destruction wrought by the barbarians, opposing a proposal to move the city to a safer place: and Rome was reborn on the same site in the first half of the 4th century B.C., being equipped above all with a massive circle of walls, which were called the Servian Walls when it was believed that they dated back to the reign of Servius Tullius. The construction of these walls, which were enormous for those times, lasted for almost a century and a half: they were built from huge square blocks of tufa stone, cut from the nearby quarries of Grotta Oscura and Fidene. The level parts reached a height of more than 30 feet and a thickness of 10, and they were reinforced on the inside by an embankment (agger) more than 100 feet thick and on the outside by a ditch more than 100 feet wide. The walls were almost 7 miles long, and took in the area which now lies between the Tiber, Piazza Venezia, Via XX Settembre, the central railway station, Piazza Vittorio Emanuele and the external slopes of the Coelian and Aventine Hills; outside the walls were the Campus Martius, Trastevere and the present-day Passeggiata Archeologica. The walls had 15 gateways, including the *Fontinalis*, through which the Via Flaminia passed, the *Collina* on the Via Salaria, the *Esquilina* giving access to the Via Casilina and Via Tiburtina and, most important of all, the *Capena*, from which the Via Appia began. Some remains of these walls can still be seen in front of the central station, in Via Carducci, Via Carlo Alberto and Viale Aventino, etc.

The structure of the city in the Republican period, as we can deduce from the writings of Cicero, was the result of spontaneous urban growth, conditioned by the characteristics of the terrain and the practical needs of the inhabitants. Real city-planning, in the modern sense of the word, did not begin until the end of the Republic, and it was made possible by two factors above all: the frequency of fires, which destroyed entire sections of the city, and the right of the emperor to deal with State-owned properties as he pleased, even without taking pre-existent monuments into consideration. In the case of Nero's fire, it has been thought that the two factors coincided, that is, that Nero deliberately set fire to the city in order to bring about a complete renovation.

In the first half of the 2nd century A.D., the appearance of Imperial Rome was that of a city with some areas which still had the old Republican structure, improved here and there, and other areas built according to a precisely co-ordinated town-planning policy. Its line of development may be briefly summarised, beginning with the period between Silla and Pompey (82-50 B.C.), which included the new appearance given to the Capitoline Hill, followed by the construction of the Tabularium, and the construction of the two bridges linking the Tiberine Island, the theatre of Pompey and the Portico of the Hundred Columns in the Campus Martius. Then came the time of Caesar (49-44 B.C.) and his reconstruction of the Roman Forum, besides the building of the Julian Basilica and the opening of the Forum of Caesar with the Temple of Venus Genetrix. This was followed by Augustus (43 B.C.-14 A.D.), with the reconstruction of dozens of temples, the opening of the Forum of Augustus with the Temple of Mars Ultor (the Vindicator), the construction of grandiose porticoes (of Octavia, of Vipsania, Saepta Julia), of the Temple of Apollo with the first Imperial residence on the Palatine, of the Ara Pacis (Altar of Peace) and of the Mausoleum of Augustus in the Campus Martius. But apart from the public buildings, the private residential areas were also designed with greater regularity.

Rome's urban development was most concentrated under the Flavians (69-96 A.D.), with the construction of the Colosseum, the transformation of the Palatine, the reorganisation of the Circus Maximus, the construction of the Stadium (Piazza Navona) and the Odeon in the Campus Martius, and the opening of the Forum of Peace, which can be considered the first museum for works of art in the ancient world. Under Nerva, Trajan and Hadrian (96-138 A.D.), the monumental character of the city is completed: this period includes the construction of the Transitory Forum with the Temple of Minerva, the Forum of Trajan, Trajan's Markets and the Baths of Trajan on the Oppian Hill, the Temple of Venus and Rome and the Mausoleum of Hadrian with the bridge called the Pons Aelius, while the Forum of Caesar, the Pantheon and the Baths of Agrippa were reconstructed.

◀ Roman Forum: marble frieze in the Basilica Aemilia.

Ancient Rome in the age of Constantine, a detail of the reconstruction model by I. Gismondi in the Museum of Roman Civilisation. (From top left: Capitolium, Circus Maximus, Imperial Fora, Palatine, Temple of Venus and Rome, Colosseum, Temple of Claudius). The population of the city grew from four hundred thousand inhabitants at the time of Silla to one million two hundred thousand in the era of Trajan.

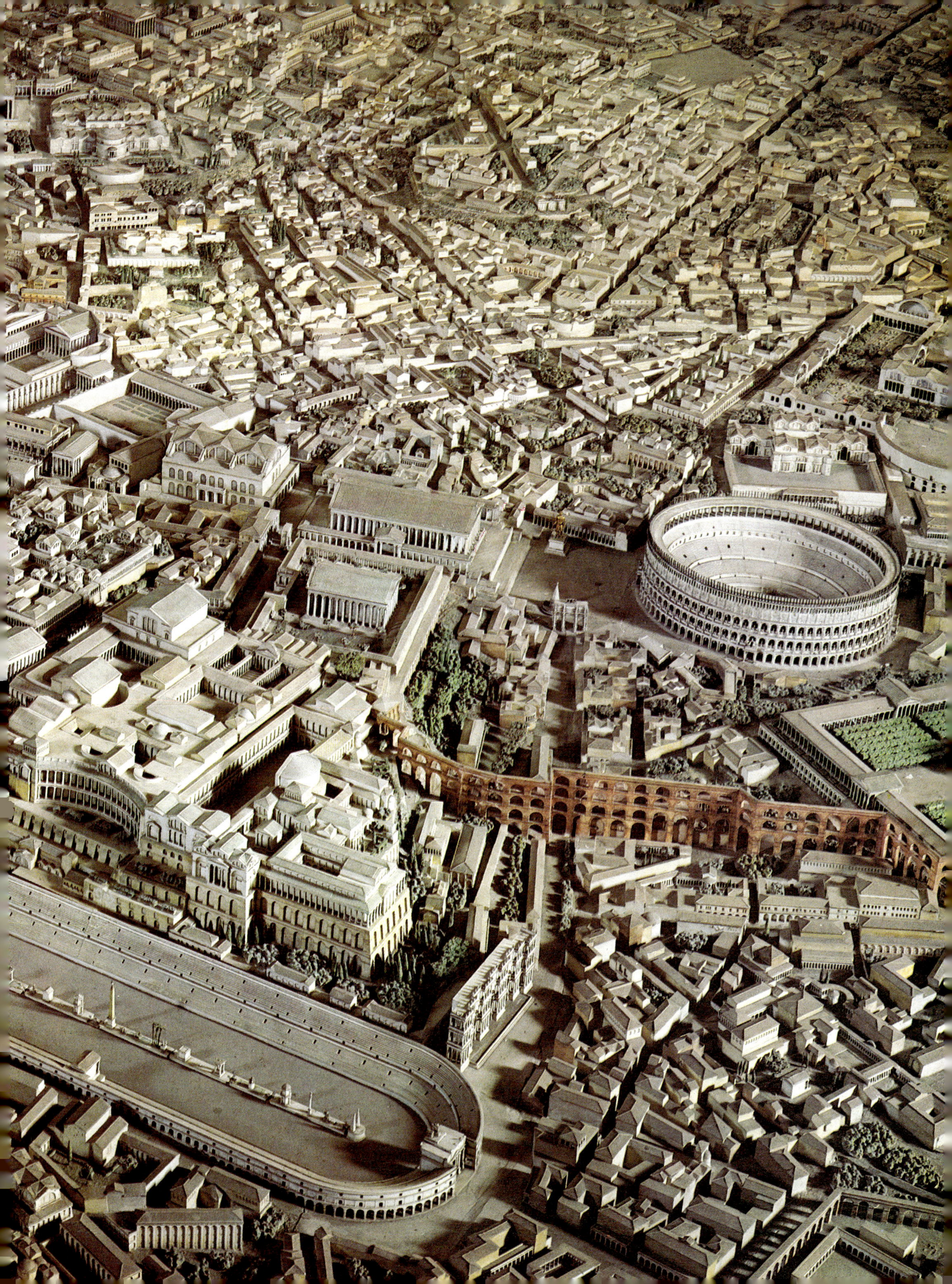

In the following century (138-235 A.D.), the Antonini and Severi emperors enriched the city with the Temple of Divus Hadrian (Piazza di Pietra), the Temple of Antoninus and Faustina, the columns of Antoninus Pius and of Marcus Aurelius, the Arch of Septimius Severus, the Severian Domus or residence and the Septizonium on the Palatine, the Castrensian amphitheatre and the Baths of Caracalla. They also reconstructed the Temple of Vesta in the Forum and the Baths of Nero in the Campus Martius. In the century between the Severi and Constantine (235-337 A.D.), Aurelian built new city walls to oppose the barbarian incursions, and the city saw the construction of the Baths of Diocletian, the Basilica of Maxentius, the Arch of Constantine, the Baths of Constantine on the Quirinal and finally the first Christian basilicas, which marked the rise of a new civilisation, after the barbarian invasions and internal warring, earthquakes and fires had inflicted irreparable damages on the city and its monuments.

In the architecture and town-planning of Rome, the three principles laid down by Vitruvius can be found: *firmitas, utilitas, venustas* (solidity, utility, beauty). For solidity, he recommends deep foundations and the correct choice of material; for utility, the choice of convenient and appropriate sites and suitable orientation, avoiding obstacles which might impede the sites' use; for beauty, a pleasant and elegant appearance and the co-ordination of the parts by exact calculations of symmetry. These three principles are demands respected by any healthy architecture, but above all by Roman architecture, so that beauty is not an ornament applied without coherency to the architectural structure but rather is bound to it and above all often represents an expression of solidity and rationality. A typical example is the Colosseum: in this monument, beauty is not achieved by sacrificing its functional character, but instead is created along with this.

Again according to Vitruvius, city squares should be in proportion to the population, so that their space does not seem too small for the people's needs nor too large if the population is scanty.

The aesthetic nature of Roman town-planning is defined by its spatial conception, whereby an architectural work clearly circumscribes its space and this in a sense creates it: in Greek architecture, the building is generally conceived as a function of the exterior, in Roman architecture as a function of the interior. Thus whereas in the Greece of the classical age we can see monumental complexes (sanctuaries, the Acropolis of Athens, etc.) in which every individual building has a value as a work of art complete in itself, in Roman town-planning the relationship between buildings is co-ordinated in such a way as to create spatial unities; areas are virtually circumscribed, indeed squares are created almost like enormous peristyles, and buildings are constructed not isolated in space and visible from every side but often placed in such a way that only one façade is visible. This tendency becomes clear above all in the temple, which stands on a base having a stairway in front. This spatial sense of architecture brings with it the grandiose dimensions: works such as the baths areas, the Pantheon and the Basilica of Maxentius are immense creations of closed space.

The evolution of architecture is linked to the development of construction techniques. Square work, consisting of blocks (first of tufa, after the middle of the 2nd century B.C. also of travertine, later of marble as well) cut into cubes, was a system used from the age of the kings up until the end of the ancient world: it permitted the building of solid, imposing structures (the Republican city walls, bases of temples, and so on). Cement work (concrete) was used from the 3rd century B.C. as the inner nucleus of square-work structures, then later in all the other techniques, beginning with the so-called uncertain work, which had a facing of small blocks irregular in form. Uncertain work appears already in the Aemilian Portico in the first half of the 2nd century B.C., and from the middle of the 1st century B.C. it becomes gradually more regular until it assumes the pattern of crossing diagonals called reticulated work, which consists of small blocks with a square base. At the end of the 1st century B.C., cement work combined with the facings of uncertain and reticulated work allowed the construction of vaults and arches and was an indispensable factor in the most daring constructions at the end of the Republic and during the Augustan age. Reticulated work came to be used less after the Augustan age: it was still seen, but with framings and strips of brick (mixed work), in the period between Trajan and the Antonini.

From the 1st century A.D., brickwork (bricks baked in kilns) asserted itself, and because of its practical advantages and solidity it soon took the place of all the other techniques. Brickwork, which reached its highest level of perfection in the age of Trajan, was the technique which — combined with the other two great triumphs of Roman building, the exploitation of the principle of the keystone in vaults and the monolithic structure obtained by the use of concrete casting (bag finish) — made possible the enormous development of Roman architecture. It permitted the covering of large spaces with massive vaults and the erection of the most daring and durable buildings ever produced by the genius of man. In fact, all the architecture of the Middle Ages and more recent times, right up until the introduction of iron into building structures and thus almost to our own day, depends on the Roman construction techniques of the arch and vault, bricks and concrete. Among the triumphs achieved by the brickwork technique, we should also mention the transformation of the private dwelling from the house with atrium, containing one family, the origins of which are estremely ancient, into the building with several storeys (as many as five), with courtyards, porticoes and shops, which accomodated a large number of families: the true ancestor of the collective habitations of our own times.

THE PALATINE

The Palatine is the hill on which the city of Rome, the "square city", was born. And on this hill we can still see the very ancient traces which are identified with the origins of Rome. In fact the bases of a group of huts recently discovered on the south part of the hill confirm the tradition that Rome was born on this hill in 753 B.C. The plan of these huts was rectangular, their corners were rounded, and the walls and covering of the roof must have been made of branches and twigs covered with dried mud. During the Imperial period, one of these huts was held in great consideration, almost worshipped, because it was believed to be the hut of the founder of Rome, Romulus (Tugurium Romuli). The choice of this hill by the primitive peoples was due to its privileged position: 160 feet above sea level and 130 feet above the level of the Tiber, it constituted a natural refuge which could be easily defended.

The hill consisted of three summits: the Palatium to the south-east towards the Circus Maximus, the Germalus to the west towards the Velabrum, and the Velia towards the Colosseum.

Fom the Republican period to the Imperial age it was considered a residential zone and the wealthiest and most noble Roman families lived there. We know that among those who dwelt there were the great rival of Cicero, Hortensius, the fabulously wealthy Crassus, Catiline, Claudius and many others. Augustus was born in 63 B.C. on the Palatine, and this was perhaps a crucial factor for the building development which took place in the Imperial age here and which eventually levelled the three hills. It was only after the victory of Actium (31 B.C.) that the emperor decided to build a dwelling worthy of his greatness, and in order to do so the adjacent areas had to be expropriated. The residence was inaugurated with a solemn ceremony on 14 January 26 B.C., but unfortunately Augustus' new dwelling was destroyed by fire in 3 A.D. When this fact became known in the provinces of the Empire, an incredible sum of money was gathered from citizens of every social class to provide for the construction of a new residence. Although Augustus accepted only a single coin from each contributor, the sum was without doubt considerable, and a new sumptuous dwelling rose on the ruins of the previous residence. Work continued until after the death of Augustus (14 A.D.). Tiberius added a new wing, the " Domus Tiberiana ", looking over the Velabrum. Caligula erected huge structures to create the space necessary for his " Domus ", between the " Domus " of Tiberius and the Forum. Claudio and Nero continued to build on the south-eastern side of the hill, where the Colosseum was later to be erected. But it was Domitian who constructed the most magnificent dwelling: the " Domus Augustana ", dwelling of the emperor and his court.

Trajan continued the building activity on the Palatine by enlarging the structures there, while Septimius Severus enlarged the southern side of the hill artificially, with a series of large brickwork arcades, constructing his baths and a great platform from which he could watch the spectacles in the Circus Maximus. From what remains, it is difficult to realise how many buildings, with terraces, porticoes, peristyles and halls, were erected here. Each emperor modified, enlarged, destroyed and rebuilt what his predecessor had created. Nevertheless, from the evidence left by Suetonius, the " House of Livia ", the original dwelling of Augustus, can be identified with certainty. Its large atrium, triclinium and wings can still be seen, as well as paintings in the second style, large panels containing figures, landscapes, perspective effects and festoons. But we know that the most important works constructed by Augustus were the Temple of Apollo, the porticoes and the libraries.

The entrance to the " Domus Pubblica " of Augustus *(Temple of Apollo)* consisted of a single arch on which stood one of the masterpieces by Lysias: a four-horse chariot driven by Apollo and Diana, sculpted from a single block of marble. After this came a large quadrangular peristyle, which had a pavement of white marble and was surrounded by old-gold columns; here were the statues of the Danaides and their father, many fragments of which were found during the excavations carried out three centuries ago. Then came the Greek and Latin libraries, divided by a great reading room, in the centre of which was a statue of the emperor with the attributes of Apollo. We know that the library of Augustus contained " books " on civil law and on the liberal arts. At the centre of the quadriporticus, between the libraries and the colonnade, stood the Temple of Apollo, built from the marble of Carrara (central Italy). The door of the temple was decorated with ivory bas-reliefs depicting the slaughter of the Niobides on one side and the expulsion of the Galatians from Delphi on the other. On the pediment was the chariot of Apollo in bronze, and inside were the statues of Apollo, a work by Scopas (4th century B.C.), Latona and Diana. Other works of

Imperial Palace on the Palatine: the Domus Augustana and the Domus Severiana seen from the Circus Maximus (at left) and the peristyle with fountain in maze form in the Domus Flavia (at right).

art are mentioned by Pliny, among them the bronze candelabra, objects of great historical value in that they had belonged to Alexander the Great (330 B.C.). Finally, we know that there were collections of splendid cameos and engraved gems, of which there are still some examples in museums.

This, according to Propertius (1st century B.C.), was the " Vestibulum " of the Palace of Augustus, which occupied a small part of the hill and of which very little has come down to us, because the whole structure was built into the new Imperial palace, constructed under Domitian and perhaps planned by his architect Rabirius. The new Imperial residence was completed in 92 A.D.: it consists of three parts, the " Domus Flavia " (Flavian Palace), the " Domus Augustana " (Imperial Palace) and the Palatine Stadium.

The Domus Flavia, the official or reception building, had a great entrance facing north with a solemn portico, and at the centre was the Throne Room with 12 niches in which there were statues made from black basalt (two are in the Museum of Parma), 16 columns of " pavonazzetto " marble and a large apse in which the Imperial throne stood. On the left was the Basilica, with yellow columns which divided it into a nave and two aisles and an apse: here legal causes were heard before the emperor. On the right was the *Lararium* or private chapel. (Beneath these areas have been found traces of the Temple of Isis, belonging to the time of Caligula). From the Throne Room, one passed out into a large peristyle with an octagonal fountain in the centre. Through the peristyle one could reach the triclinium with its apse in which was the Imperial couch. Traces have been preserved of the magnificent polychrome marble pavement here. This area was built with a splendid scenographic effect: on one side it opened onto the peristyle and on the other two sides there were large openings onto two nymphaea (fountain areas), oval in form. The harmonious structure was completed by a large portico towards the Circus Maximus and two libraries mentioned by Suetonius.

The second section, the Domus Augustana or private residence of the emperor and his family, was divided into two storeys; the upper storey was on the same level as the reception building and had a vast central peristyle with a fountain or impluvium in the middle; the lower storey had a second portico, around which were the rooms of the private dwelling, many of which had large openings looking over the valley of the Circus Maximus.

The third section, completing Domitian's plan, was the Stadium or Racecourse. It was surrounded by porticoes decorated with half-columns towards the arena and with one or two galleries above. It measured 175 yards by 55 yards. Still to be seen are the turning posts and many fragments of columns and capitals besides a square-shaped altar on which are depicted the 12 divinities of Olympus: Minerva, Juno, Mars and so on. The Imperial stand (pulvinar) consisted of a large exedra divided into two floors; the emperor sat on the second floor, from which he could watch the spectacles and admire the overall view of this splendid architectural complex.

Behind the Stadium of Domitian are the remains of the Baths of Septimius Severus (203 A.D.). In order to build them, the entire southern corner of the hill had to be lengthened by constructing a series of massive brickwork arcades with several storeys (already prepared in part by Domitian), which went as far as the seating area of the Circus Maximus itself. The baths terminated on the southern side in a large scenic platform from which the emperors could watch the chariot races in the circus below.

To complete the sumptuous appearance of the Imperial palaces on the Palatine, as a sort of enormous and imposing theatrical scene for those en-

Imperial Palace on the Palatine: the Palatine Stadium or racecourse, constructed by Domitian.

tering Rome by the Via Appia, Septimius Severus constructed a building called the Septizodium, after the seven planets which were depicted there. The building, in which rich use of marbles was made, had three storeys with columns, and between the columns were exedrae with artistic fountains and statues. The most precious of marbles were used in its construction, and this was perhaps the cause of its complete demolition under Pope Sixtus V in 1589, carried out by the pope's architect Fontana. It should be added that this building is often referred to by the name of Septizonium (seven zones), since it has been thought that the building itself had seven storeys.

Impressive, majestic, indeed indescribable, must have been the impression made on travellers who reached Rome along the Via Appia and who came face to face with the grandeur of the Circus Maximus, the beauty of the Septizodium and the majesty of the Imperial Palaces.

THE ROMAN FORUM

With the construction of the Cloaca Maxima, completed under the Etruscan dynasty of the Tarquins, the last kings of Rome, the swampy valley which lay between the Campidoglio, the Palatine and the slopes of the Esquiline Hill was drained and reclaimed and became the meeting-place of the inhabitants who lived on the surrounding hills. From that moment, the small valley became the *square* (the *forum*), the political, religious and commercial fulcrum of Rome: the Forum Romanum.

Processions, trials, triumphal ceremonies, political meetings and elections took place here, and in fact it was the nerve centre of Republican Rome. But it was given its monumental appearance, for the most part, by Caesar, Augustus and Tiberius. It is difficult for someone looking at the ruins for the first time today to realise its importance: nevertheless, in this square, among what are now the ruins of basilicas and temples, honorary columns and triumphal arches, men with names like Silla, Cato, Cicero, Caesar, Augustus, Tiberius and many others discussed and decided the destiny of Rome. In this square, the great adventure of the Romans, the adventure of our own civilisation, had its beginnings.

Among the numerous remains of the Forum, we shall limit our discussion to those which, more than the others, reveal and typify its three fundamental aspects: the political, the legal and administrative, and the religious aspects.

The political aspect is represented by the Curia (Senate), the Comitium and the Rostra. The origins of the *CURIA* are extremely ancient: tradition has it that it dates back to Tullus Hostilius, the third king of Rome; it was destroyed and reconstructed at various times. Julius Caesar rebuilt it completely, moving it towards the ancient Comitium and changing its orientation. The brickwork building which remains today dates from the time of Diocletian (303 A.D.). The bronze doors were removed by Pope Alexander VII and placed on the main entrance of the

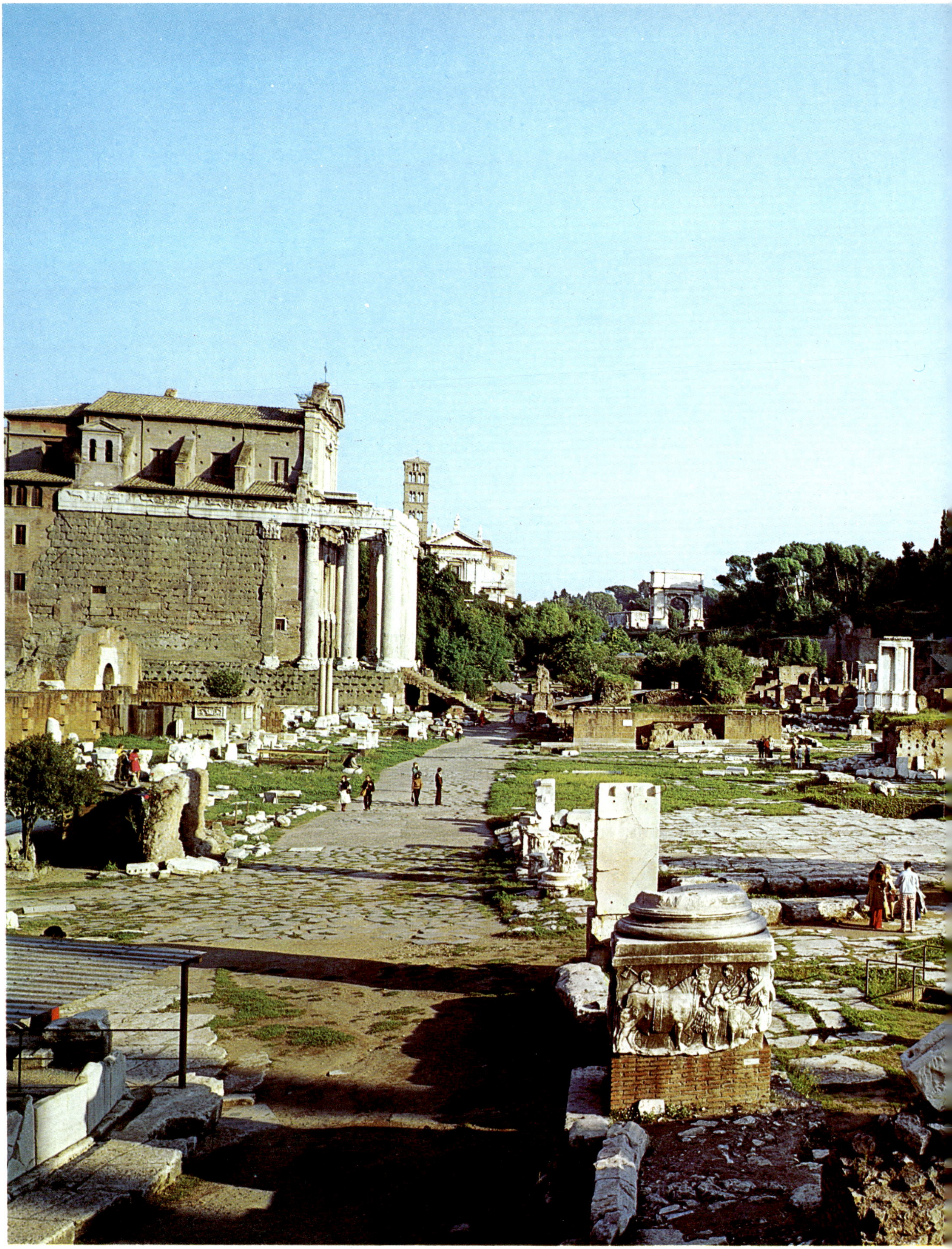

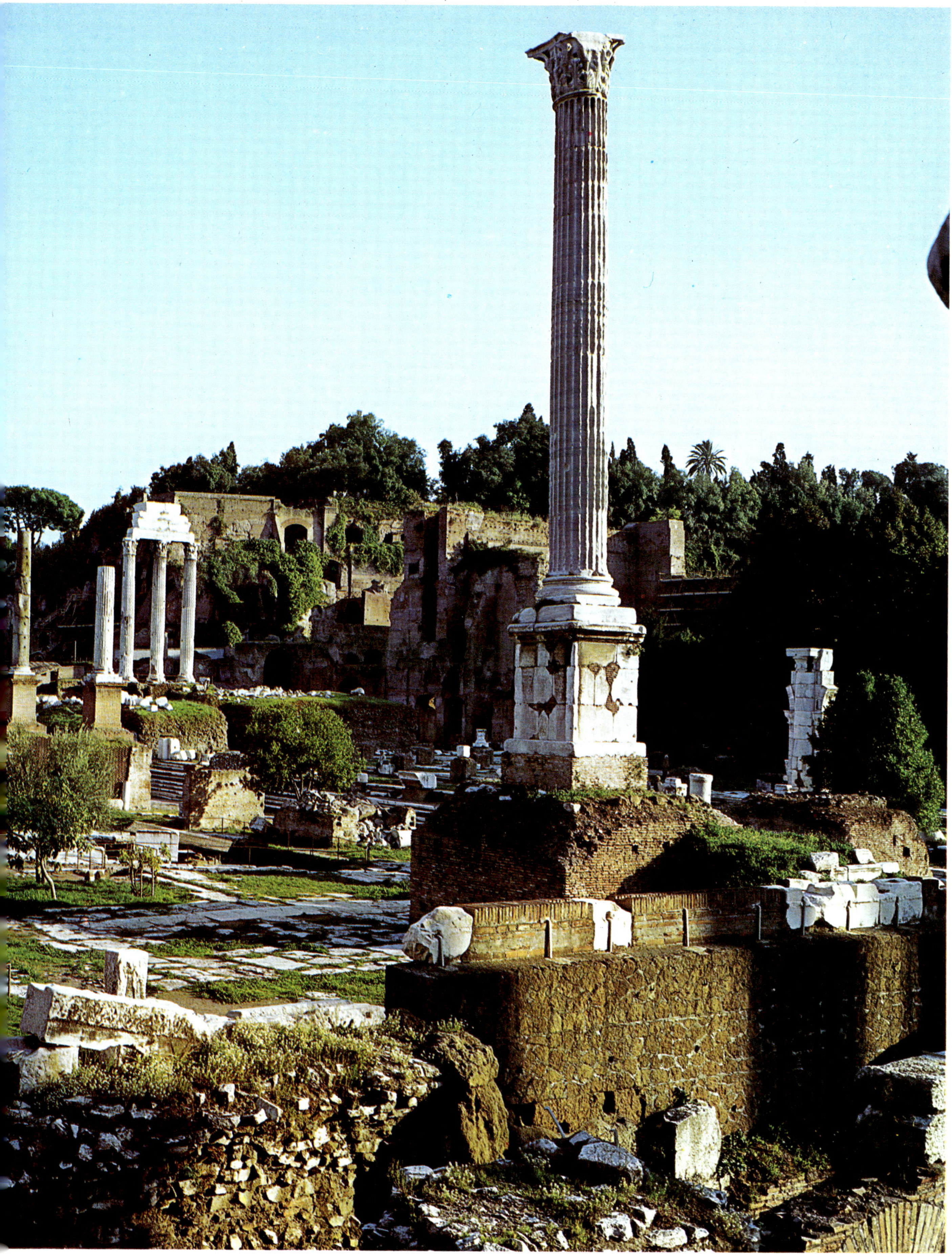

Basilica of St. John-in-Lateran. The interior of the Curia is rectangular in form (149 by 60 feet), and its walls were covered with marble slabs up to a certain height; above the marble decoration there were three niches on each side, decorated with small alabaster columns.

At the sides there were steps, which can still be seen, on which wooden seats were placed for the senators (about 300). The floor (the central part is still in a good state of preservation) consists of a marble inlay with porphyry and serpentine. In front of the entrance there must have been the altar on which the senators made sacrifices when entering the hall. On the wall opposite the entrance, there was a podium for the president and here, against the wall, was the statue of Victory. The Curia, seat of the Roman Senate, was the scene of the most decisive events in the history of Rome.

The *COMITIUM* was an area between the Senate, the Arch of Septimius Severus and the Lapis Niger, an area consecrated as a temple, where meetings for the election of the magistrates representing the common people (plebs) and demonstrations against the power exercised by the Senate were held.

The many reconstructions of the Comitium in various periods make it difficult to establish its area and original appearance. However, the Comitium and the Curia express the profound meaning epitomised by the letters S.P.Q.R.: the Senate and People of Rome.

The *ROSTRA* constituted the platform from which the political orators spoke. It was given this name because the front of it was adorned by six bronze rostra, seized by the Romans from the ships at Antium during the Latin war (338 B.C.). We know that they were decorated with columns and honorary statues (relief on the Arch of Constantine). The present situation of the rostra is that established by Julius Caesar, who placed them on the same axis as the square and the Julia and Aemilia Basilicas. Apart from the Rostra, two other podiums for political orators existed in the forum, these also equipped with rostra, one in front of the Temple of Pollux and Castor and the other in front of the Temple of Julius Caesar.

On the long sides of the Forum stood the two basilicas: the Julia to the west and the Aemilia to the east.

The Basilica Julia was begun by Julius Caesar in 54 B.C.; it consisted of a rectangular structure with a two-storey gallery around it. The façade on the Via Sacra had a two-storey portico with barrel-vaults and half-columns attached to the pillars. Destroyed by a fire, it was rebuilt and enlarged by Augustus (12 A.D.); destroyed once more by the fire of Carinus (284 A.D.), it was restored by Diocletian (303 A.D.). Finally it was destroyed still another time by the Goths led by Alaric (410 A.D.), and nothing remains of it except the paving. It was the seat of the administration of justice and the site of public meetings.

Façade of the Curia, seat of the Roman Senate, reconstructed by Diocletian (303 A.D.). Its bronze door is today the main door of the church of St. John-in-Lateran.

The Roman Forum seen from the Campidoglio (from left: Basilica Aemilia, Temple of Antoninus and Faustina, Via Sacra, Arch of Titus, base of the Decennial column, Temple of Vesta, Temple of the Dioscuri, Palace of Caligula on the Palatine, Basilica Julia, Column of Phocas).

The Basilica Aemilia was constructed in 179 B.C. by the consuls M. Aemilius Lepidus and Fulvius Nobilio. It was destroyed, only to be rebuilt, several times: in 14 B.C., in 22 A.D., and finally, by the Goths of Alaric, in 410 A.D. It was a splendid building, richly decorated with marble. It had a great portico on the front, with two orders in the Tuscan style, and a frieze with triglyphs and metopes; behind the portico there were 12 booths, six on each side of the central entranceway. It seems that at the time of Augustus the portico was removed from the structure of the basilica to form a self-contained building which was consecrated to Gaius and Lucius Caesar, the adoptive sons of Augustus. Behind the booths was the great hall of the basilica, divided by marble columns into four aisles. The first was 17 feet wide, the main aisle or nave was 39 feet wide and 262 feet long, and then came the two minor aisles so that the basilica bordered on the Forum of Nerva.

Roman Forum towards the Campidoglio, with an arch of the Basilica Julia and the pronaos of the Temple of Saturn, which contained the Treasury of the Roman people.

The Roman Forum seen from the Palatine (from left: Portico of the Gods (Dii Consentes), Tabularium, Temple of Saturn, Temple of Vespasian, Basilica Julia, Arch of Septimius Severus, Curia, Temple of the Dioscuri, Temple of Vesta, Temple of Antoninus and Faustina, Lapis Niger).

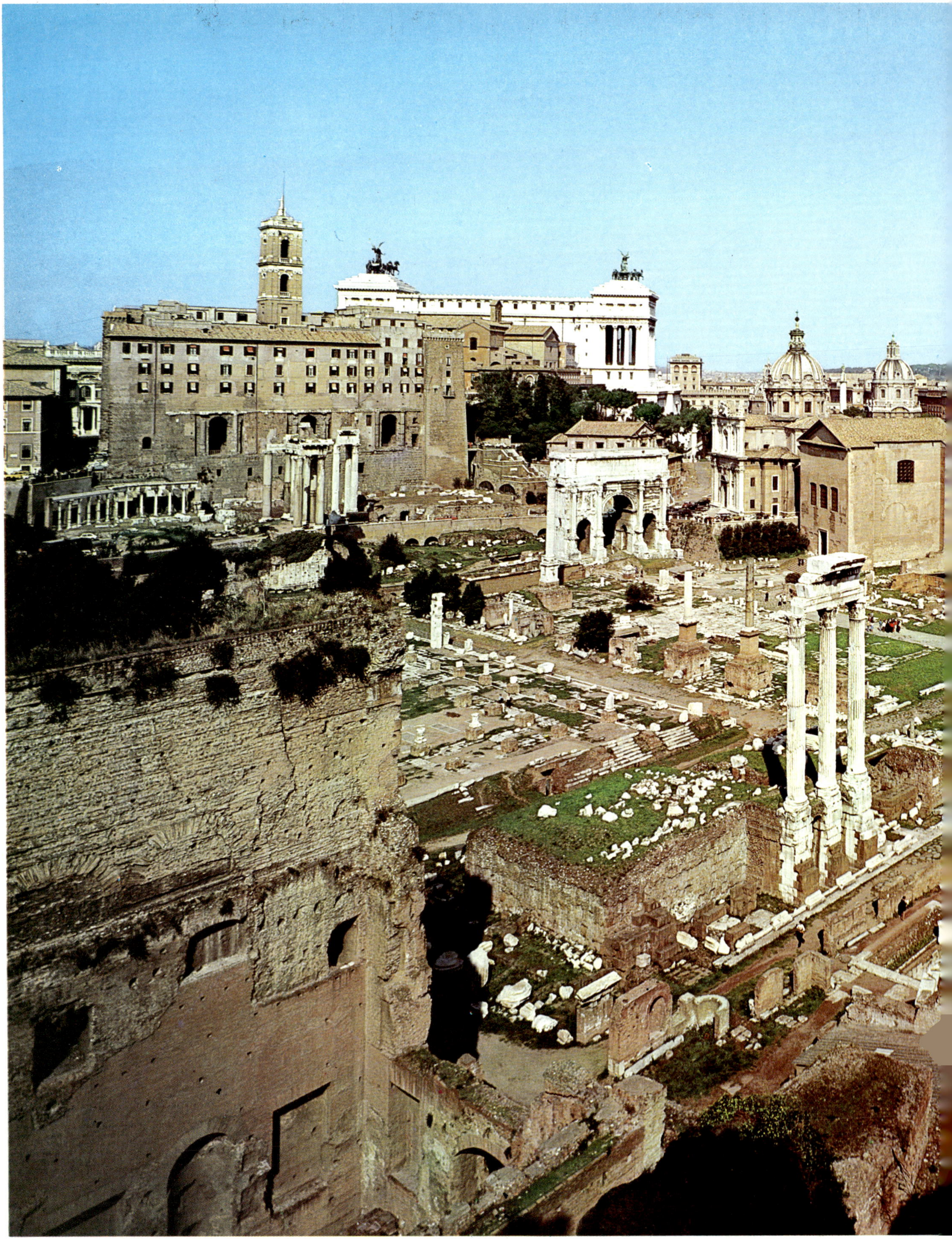

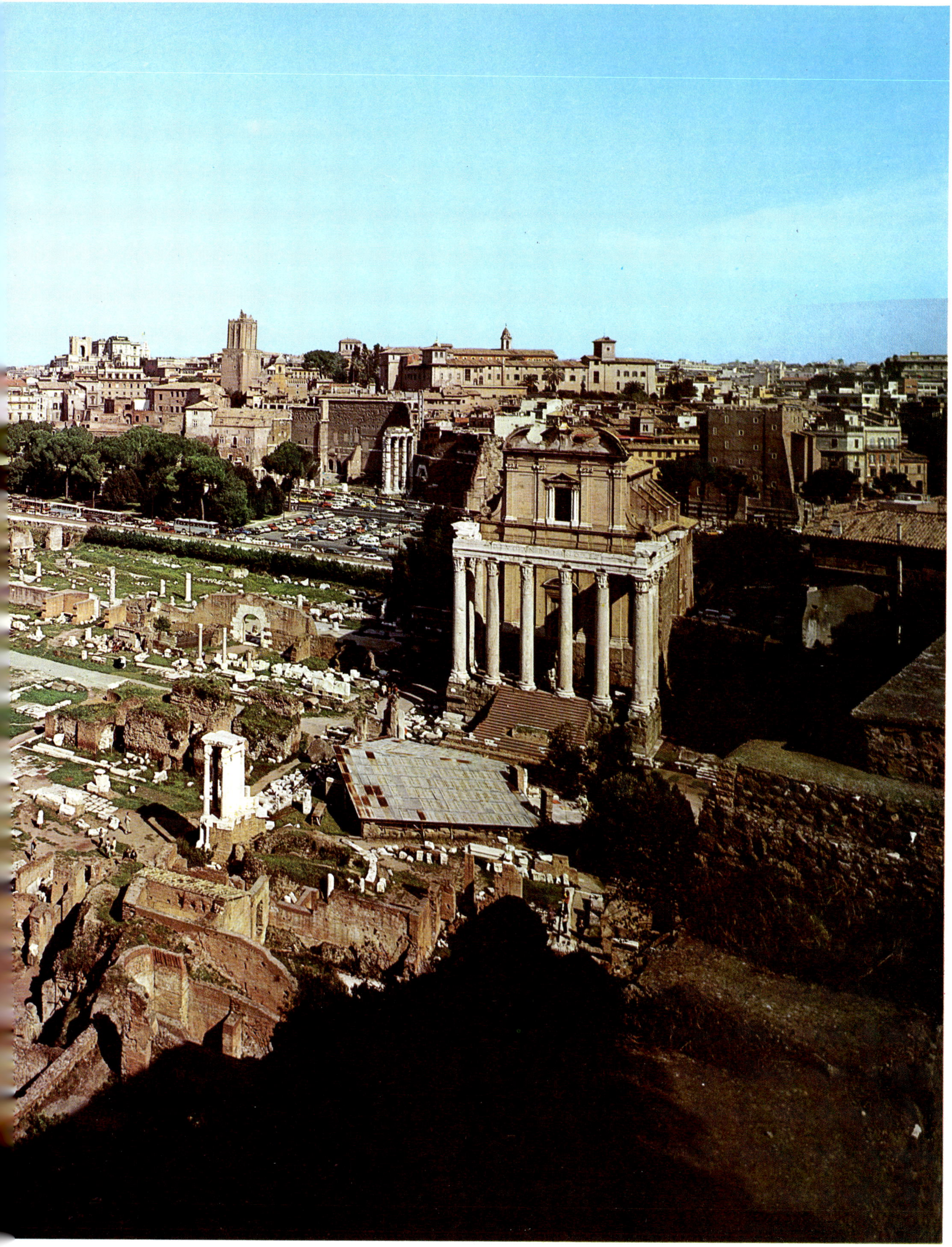

Temple of the Dioscuri in the Roman Forum: reconstruction (left) and the three columns still standing (right).

On the northern side, looking over the Via dell'Argileto which separated the basilica from the Curia, there seems to have been a door with columns on plinths at the sides and Doric trabeation with triglyphs and bucrania (ox-skull motifs). Some think that these bucrania gave the area the name of Campo Vaccino (Cow Field), which was used up to last century; but others attribute this popular nomenclature to the simple fact that the cattle market was held among the ruins of the Forum, before excavations were begun.

In front of the Basilica Aemilia was the Via Sacra, which ran lengthways through the Forum from the Temple of Saturn to the Arch of Titus. It was the first and most important street of the city, and the religious-political processions passed along it towards the Clivus Capitolinus to terminate at the Temple of Jupiter Optimus Maximus on the Campidoglio.

On the south-eastern side of the square, giving it a monumental appearance, were the three temples which in a sense summarise the religious aspect of the Forum: the Temple of Castor and Pollux, the Temple of Vesta and the Temple of Caesar. The Temple of Castor and Pollux was consecrated on 1 January 484 B.C.; it was rebuilt many times in various ages, and the present-day remains, three splendid columns with trabeation, belong to the time of Tiberius (1st century A.D.). This temple is identified with the birth of the Roman Republic and stood next to the Fountain of Juturna, where according to the legend which has come down to us from Plutarch Castor and Pollux appeared to the Romans on horseback to announce the victory won by the people against the last king of Rome at Lake Regillo. As it was reconstructed by Tiberius

(19 A.D.), the temple stood on a high podium with steps covered with marble on the front. It was an octastyle, peripteral structure (with a single row of columns, eight on the front). In the pronaos there was a " mensa ponderaria " (weighing and measuring table), possibly used by the money-changers and jewel merchants who had their shops on the summit of the Via Sacra. In the temple were the statues of Castor and Pollux, which from the time of the construction of the temple dedicated to them were considered the guardians of Rome's liberty. The temple was separated from the Basilica Julia by the *Vicus Tuscus*, which linked the Forum with the area of the Circus Maximus.

The Temple of Vesta, which stands slightly back from the square, is extremely ancient and was perhaps built by Numa Pompilius himself, the second king of Rome and the founder of the cult of Vesta. In this temple, the most important in the Forum and indeed in the city, the Vestal Virgins had custody of the Sacred Fire, symbol of the life of the city and therefore never allowed to go out. The temple was round, with an opening high up, similar to the

House of the Vestals in the Roman Forum: reconstruction (right) and view of the courtyard (below).

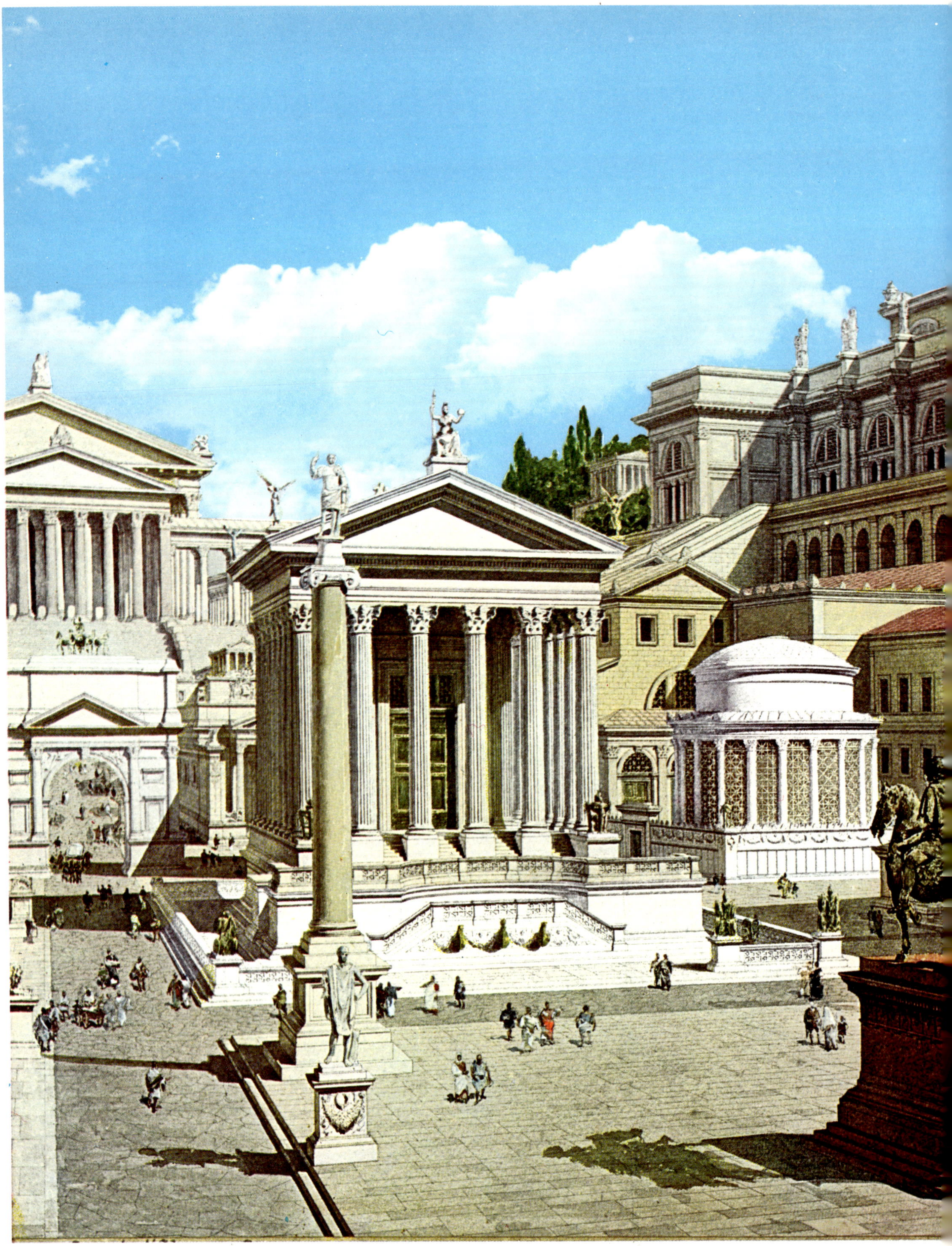

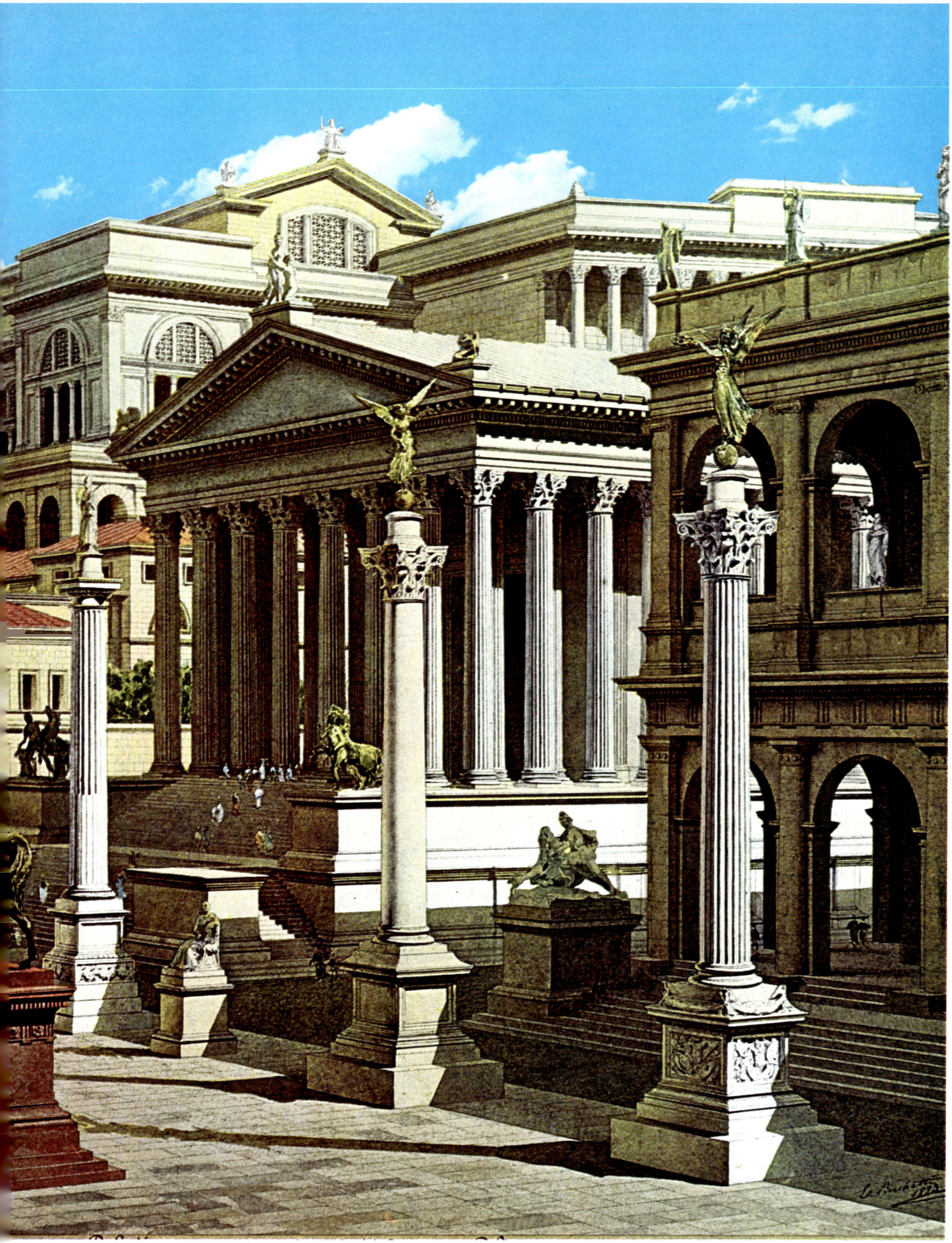

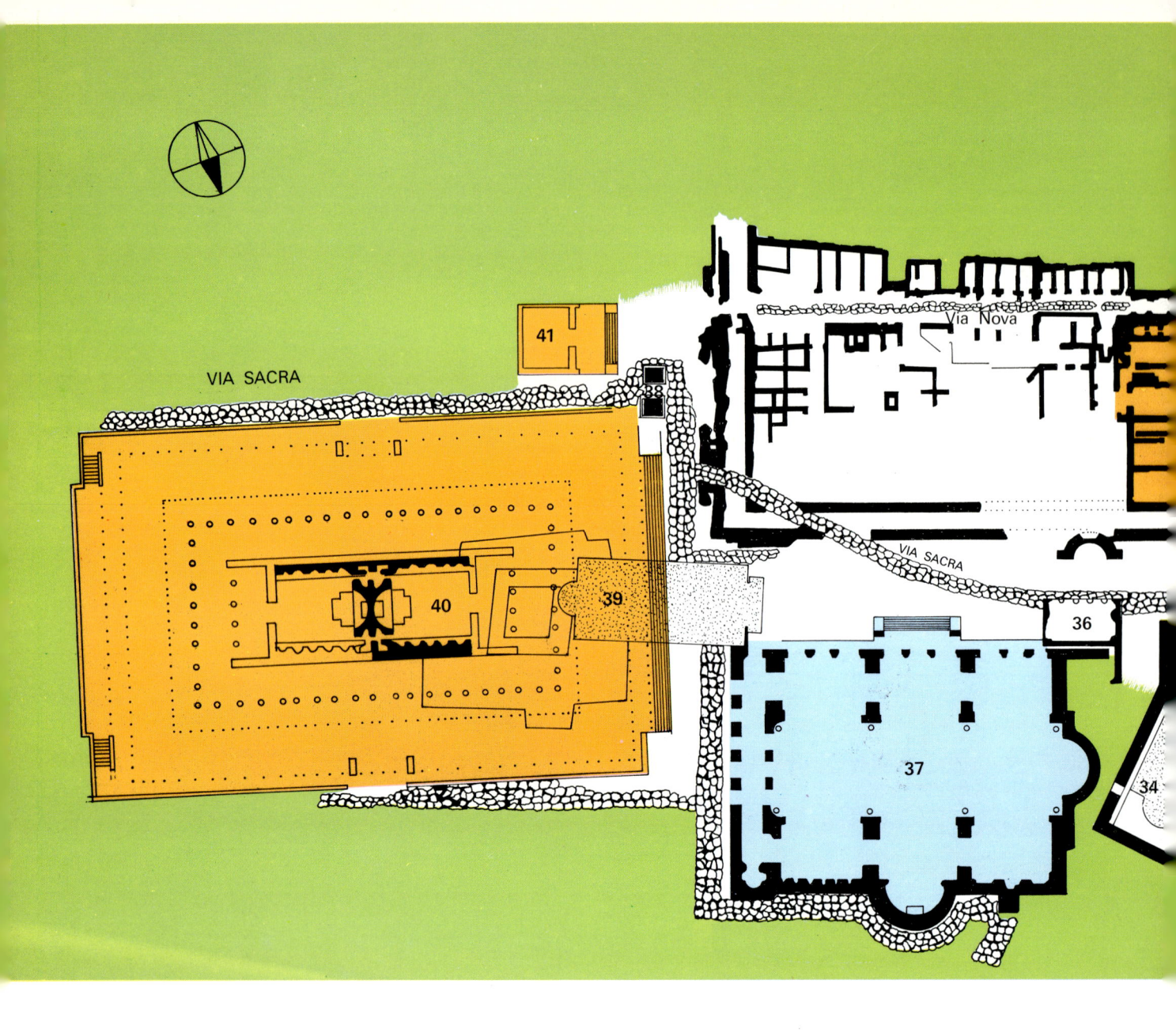

THE ROMAN FORUM

◀ Reconstruction of the Roman Forum seen from the Campidoglio (from left: Temple of Julius Caesar, Temple of Vesta, Temple of the Dioscuri, honorary columns, corner of the Basilica Julia; in the background the Palace of Caligula on the Palatine).

Religious buildings

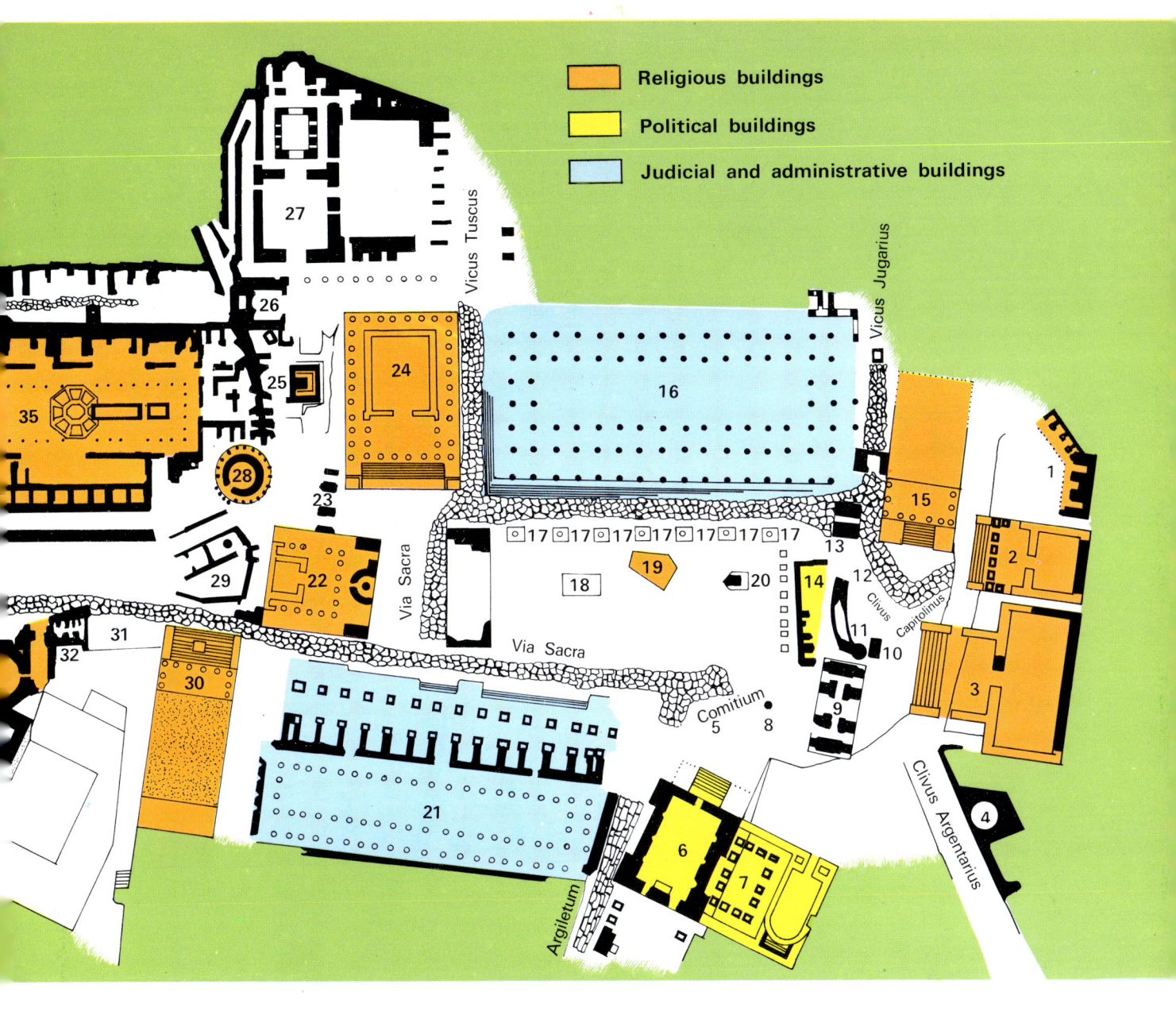

Political buildings

Judicial and administrative buildings

KEY

1 PORTICO OF THE DII CONSENTES
2 TEMPLE OF VESPASIAN
3 TEMPLE OF CONCORD
4 MAMERTINE PRISON
5 COMITUM
6 CURIA
7 SECRETARIUM SENATI
8 LAPIS NIGER
9 ARCH OF SEPTIMIUS SEVERUS
10 ALTAR OF VULCAN
11 UMBILICUS URBIS ROMAE
12 MILIARIUM AUREUM
13 ARCH OF TIBERIUS
14 ROSTRUM OF THE CAESARS
15 TEMPLE OF SATURN
16 BASILICA JULIA
17 HONORARY COLUMNS
18 EQUESTRIAN STATUE OF DOMITIAN
19 LACUS CURTIUS
20 COLUMN OF PHOCAS
21 BASILICA AEMILIA
22 TEMPLE OF CAESAR
23 ARCH OF AUGUSTUS
24 TEMPLE OF THE DIOSCURI
25 SHRINE AND FOUNTAIN OF JUTURNA
26 ORATORY OF THE FORTY MARTYRS
27 BIBLIOTHECA PACIS (CHURCH OF S. MARIA ANTIQUA)
28 TEMPLE OF VESTA
29 REGIA
30 TEMPLE OF ANTONINUS AND FAUSTINA
31 PRE ROMAN BURIAL-GROUNDS
32 INN
33 TEMPLE OF ROMULUS
34 CHURCH OF SS. COSMA AND DAMIAN
35 HOUSE OF THE VESTALS
36 MEDIEVAL PORTICO
37 BASILICA OF MAXENTIUS AND CONSTANTINE
38 ARCH OF TITUS
39 CHURCH OF S. FRANCESCA ROMANA
40 TEMPLE OF VENUS AND ROME
41 TEMPLE OF JUPITER STATOR

primitive hut dwellings. It stood on a square base next to the House of the Vestals and was separated from the Regia, residence of the Pontifex, by a small street branching off the Via Sacra: the *Vicus Vestae*. The temple as we see it today, only a small part of the original, dates from the last restoration, or rather reconstruction, carried out by order of the wife of Septimius Severus, Julia Domna, towards 204 A.D.

The Pontifex Maximus was considered the spiritual head of the Vestals, but a the same time he had no part in the practice of the cult, which was the exclusive duty of the six Vestal Virgins, chosen from among the noblest families of the city. These women had to take vows of chastity and continued to fulfil their duties for thirty years. The privileges enjoyed by the priestesses of Vesta were numerous, but the punishment inflicted if a Vestal failed in her

The Temple of Vesta in the Roman Forum: reconstruction from an ancient relief.

duty or broke her vow of chastity was terrible: she was buried alive. Tragic and explicit is the description of the sentencing to death of a Vestal, which has come down to us from Plutarch: " The unfortunate guilty woman is carried on a funeral car, to which she is bound with straps of leather, through the Forum, the Vicus Longus and Alta Semita (High Path) as far as the Porta Collina. The crowd opens in silence to let the funeral procession pass: not a word is heard, not a single lament. Silent tears fall from the eyes of every spectator. Finally the procession reaches a point near the opening of a crypt, the high priest raises his arms towards the Gods, the unfortunate guilty woman descends by means of a ladder into the tomb. As soon as she has descended into the crypt, the ladder is removed, the opening is closed with a huge stone and a large quantity of earth is heaped over it so as to cancel all trace of the tragic site ."

Finally, virtually closing off the south-eastern side of the square, there was the Temple of Julius Caesar. Of this building, only the part forming the cement work, that is, the internal structure of the podium, has survived to our time; the entire upper, architectural part has disappeared. It had an Ionic, hexastyle (six-columned) pronaos. The podium did not have steps as was customary, but instead a wall projecting from the row of columns which served as a platform for orators (Rostra Nova). In the wall of the podium were placed the rostra which Augustus had seized from the ships of Mark Antony and Cleopatra in the famous Battle of Actium (31 B.C.).

The ruins which can still be seen at the centre of the niche in the podium have been identified by recent studies as the Altar of Caesar. Here Mark Antony delivered the funeral oration in honour of Caesar. The words of Antony have been lost, but perhaps, given the inspired intuition of that great poet Shakespeare, we may be permitted to say that the words of the poet could have been the words of Antony:

" Friend, Romans, countrymen, lend me your ears;
I come to bury Caesar, not to praise him.
The evil that men do lives after them,
The good is oft interred with their bones ".

Between the Temple of Castor and Pollux and the Temple of Caesar, standing astride the Vicus Vestae as if to form the monumental entrance to the square, was the Arch of Augustus, with three barrel-vaults of which the central one was larger

The Temple of Vesta in the Roman Forum: restored section, from the Severian age.

28

than the side ones. On the attic were two statues of soldiers and a four-horse chariot, and in the vaults were affixed the *Fasti Consulari* (Consular Annals), now in the Capitoline Museum. We know that this arch was dedicated in the year 29 B.C. to the victory of Actium (31 B.C.).

To complete the description of the overall appearance of the Forum, one must of course mention the decorative elements with which it was enriched over the centuries, such as the triumphal arches of Tiberius and Septimius Severus; the innumerable statues, including the famous equestrian statue of Domitian which stood in the middle of the square; the honorary columns, of which we have the bases and important fragments; the sacred places of ancient memory such as the Lapis Niger, the Sacellum, or chapel, of Venus Cloacina; the Temple of Janus; the Umbilicus Urbis, which marked the central point of the city, and the Miliarum Aureum, which served to measure the distance from Rome to the provinces of the Empire. Finally there were the shops and booths and sanitary services, as well as fountains and marble constructions.

The Forum was always, even during the Imperial period when the many monuments had made it extremely crowded and when other, more spacious Fora had been opened, the real heart of the city: from the early hours of the day, a multitude of people flowed into it — some for legal cases, others for commercial reasons, others as part of the retinue of important political figures, others again simply to meet their friends.

Basilica of Maxentius in the Roman Forum: the three arches on the north side (above) and reconstruction (below).

Temple of Venus and Rome, built to a design by the emperor Hadrian. It consists of two temples with facing cellae (chambers), and alongside it are porticoes which thus create a new Forum between the Roman Forum and the Colosseum.

CAMPIDOGLIO

The Campidoglio was the natural fortress of Rome. Its occupation by the Romans was a necessary step in the development of Rome and indeed in its very existence. The strategic position of the Campidoglio made it a bulwark with respect to both river and overland communications: dominating the Tiber on one side and the Valley of the Forum on the other, it allowed the Romans to cut off anyone who wanted either to cross or to travel up the river, and at the same time offered a natural link with the sea. The Latins, the Sabines and the Etruscans all had to succumb to or be absorbed by this rising new power.

The hill had two summits, north and south, with a depression between them. The northern summit was fortified from the earliest beginnings of Rome; it was the *Arx*, the perfect stronghold. The southern height was called the *Capitolium*, a name which seems to have been due to the discovery of a large human skull *(caput)*. The depression between the two summits was called the *Asylum*.

The most important monument was built on the summit of the Capitolium; this was the temple dedicated to the Capitoline Triad, the Temple of Jupiter Optimus Maximus. For this reason it was always the object of special attention. Destroyed several times by fire, it was on each occasion rebuilt richer and more magnificent than ever. The original temple seems to have been consecrated by Tarquinius Priscus and completed by Tarquin the Proud, and in any case it was inaugurated, according to what the historian Livy tells us, in 509 B.C., the first year in the life of the Roman Republic. Like the Etruscan temples, the temple had three chambers. The walls and columns were made of tufa, while the covering was of wood overlaid with sheets of terracotta. In the central chamber there was a terracotta statue of Jupiter, the work of Vulca, the great artist from the

◀ The Campidoglio in ancient times: reconstruction model (at left, the Temple of Jupiter at the time of Domitian; at right, the Temple of Juno Moneta).

The Campidoglio today. At the sides of the ramp, the two groups of the Dioscuri, from the late Imperial period.

Etruscan city of Veii. In the lateral chambers were the statues of Juno and Minerva respectively. The statue of Jupiter had the symbolic thunderbolt in its right hand, the face was painted red and it was dressed in precious fabrics.

On the roof of the temple was a terracotta group depicting Jupiter triumphant in a four-horse chariot, this too a work by Vulca of Veii. In the temple were kept the splendid spoils of victories and votive offerings. The temple was rebuilt on numerous occasions (by Silla in 83 B.C., Augustus in 26 B.C., Vespasian in 75 A.D. and Domitian in 82 A.D.). In the final version, the statue of Jupiter was of gold and ivory like the Zeus of Olympia. The temple was completely covered with marble, a fact which was to save it from further destruction by fire. Above the pediment were the acroteria, or pedestals, which supported the bronze four-horse chariot of Jupiter in the centre and those of Minerva and Mars at the sides. The columns were of white Pentelic marble, the roof was covered with gilt bronze tiles and the doors were covered with gold sheets. These precious materials were carried off by the barbarian hordes led by the Goth kings. Today, in the Palazzo dei Conservatori, only the grandiose remains of its stylobate (basement of the columns) and fragments of the columns can be seen. The main entrance to the Capitoline area was on the south-eastern side, towards the Forum, reached by the Capitoline *Clivus* (slope), where the Tabularium, or State Archive, stood. In and around the Temple zone there were numerous small temples altars, shrines and porticoes, the exact position of which is not known. There were also innumerable statues, busts of generals and emperors. The area was so crowded with these that Augustus had them removed and transported to a new part of the city, the Campus Martius. There were also several triumphal arches, among them that of Scipio the African, decorated with seven gilt bronze statues. On the northern summit, above the

The "Mosaic of the Doves", found in Hadrian's Villa (Capitoline Museum). Done in the most highly perfected technique (opus vermiculatum), it was probably inspired by a famous original belonging to the art of Pergamon, mentioned by Pliny.

Equestrian monument to Marcus Aurelius (161-180 A.D.), previously in the Lateran, brought to the Campidoglio in 1538. It is the only equestrian monument of an emperor which has come down to our times.

33

fortress, stood the ancient temple dedicated to Juno Moneta (244 B.C.).

The Campidoglio was thus both symbol and guardian of the religious and political powers of Rome.

Today the Campidoglio, risen from the ruins thanks to the genius of Michelangelo and his successors, has perhaps no need to envy its glorious past: the square with the majestic equestrian statue of Marcus Aurelius in the centre and the buildings at the sides which frame it and create a sense of perspective, forms an oasis of architectural perfection whose reputation for perennial beauty can only be preserved with the passing of time. But what contributes to the Campidoglio's millenial importance is the fact that, apart from being the official seat of the Mayor and of the Administration of the city, it is also the site of the oldest museum in the world (1471).

It was Pope Sixtus IV who, as the commemorative inscription recalls, decided to restore several exceptional bronze statues to the Roman people, who had created them. These statues are the She-wolf, the Camillus, the Boy with the Thorn and a head once said to be of Domitian but which has been shown since to be of Constantius II. In 1566, Pius V donated to the museum more than 30 statues taken from the Vatican, and later other works again. In 1714, Clement XI gave the Campidoglio five Egyptian statues found in the vicinity of the Porta Salaria. The year 1733 was an important one for the museum, because it was then that the collection of Cardinal Alessandro Albani was bought, including the portraits now in the Sala degli Imperatori and the Sala dei Filosofi. Under Pope Clement XII the museum acquired one of its finest pieces, the Dying Gaul. Then, thanks to Benedict XIV, the Picture Gallery was created. In 1750 the Capitoline Venus was acquired and in 1765 the Mosaic of the Doves and two Centaurs of grey marble, found at Hadrian's Villa, were bought. In 1734 the museum was opened to the public, and since then it has continued to enlarge its collections.

The collections of the Capitoline Museum, whether they be of marble or bronze, paintings or mosaics, gather together works which all come from Rome. This is what gives the collections not only a sense of unity but also a definite role as the "Treasury of Rome".

The "Capitoline Venus", from a Greek original of the 4th-3rd century B.C. (Capitoline Museum).

Sculptures in the Capitoline Museum: above, statue of the Dying Galatian, from a Pergamon original of the 3rd century B.C.; below, sarcophagus with scenes of battle between Greeks and Galatians, from the 2nd century A.D.

35

The "Capitoline She-Wolf", Etruscan sculpture of the 5th century B.C., with the Twins added by Pollaiolo (Museo dei Conservatori).

From left: Bronze portrait of the 3rd century B.C., called the "Capitoline Brutus" (Museo dei Conservatori). Female portrait from the end of the 1st century A.D. Bust of the emperor Commodus (180-192 A.D.), depicted as Hercules (Capitoline Museum).

RELIGION AND THE TEMPLES

The ancient temple on the Campidoglio derived not only architecturally but also in its rituals from Etruria, since it was dedicated to the Triad of Jupiter, Juno and Minerva; but it was called for short the Temple of Jupiter, or of Capitoline Jupiter, or simply the *Capitolium*. Throughout the ancient era it remained the most important temple in the city and became the supreme symbol of the Roman spirit, so much so that each Roman municipality in Italy and in the provinces had its own *Capitolium*.

The Roman religion, just as it had welcomed from the beginning the Etruscan triad, so during the course of the centuries generously adopted the divinities of all the people who became part of the civilisation of Rome; indeed, the Greek divinities, which were already famous in literature and art, were assimilated with the old Italic divinities, which had a completely different character. Thus Hera became Juno, Athene was turned into Minerva, Ares into Mars, Aphrodite into Venus, and so on; only Apollo remained as he had been in Greek mythology. Thus the Greek Olympus became the Roman Olympus, which was further enriched by many other foreign divinities, such as the Magna Mater (Cybele) who had her temple on the Palatine, Isis who had a large sanctuary built in the Egyptian style in the Campus Martius, the oriental divinities whose sanctuary has been discovered on the Janiculum, and finally Mithras, the Persian God of the Sun, whose worship, which included initiations, mysteries and symbolic ceremonies, spread more

Temples in the Forum Boarium: at left, round temple from the 1st century B.C., wrongly said to be of Vesta; at right, rectangular temple of the Republican era, called the Temple of Fortuna Virilis.

than any other cult (Mithraic sanctuaries have been found under S. Prisca, under the Baths of Caracalla, under San Clemente, under the Palazzo Barberini, at Ostia).

New divinities, which we might call political, also became part of this Olympus: the Goddess Rome, Concordia, the deified Augustus and the other emperors who had proved themselves deserving of deification, such as the Divus Vespasian, the Divus Titus, the Divus Trajan and the Divus Hadrian; and then there was above all the divinity Peace, to which, after the monumental Altar erected under Augustus, a large temple and even a Forum under the Flavians were dedicated.

All these divinities, the old and the new, Etruscan, Italic, Greek, Oriental and typically Roman, created that religious " sincretism " which served as a distant preparation for the advent of Christianity.

From an architectural point of view, the Roman temples used, as an analogy to the variety and diversity of the cults, various different solutions and elements: the Greek models were modified and enriched in their decorations, in which the Corinthian style prevailed, and the composite style was created (Corinthian-Ionic), while the Tuscan style, which already represented a fusion of Doric and Etruscan motifs, was maintained and developed.

The Ara Pacis Augustae (Altar of Peace of Augustus), erected between 19 and 13 B.C. on the Via Lata, now Via del Corso; reconstructed by G. Moretti in 1938.

Alongside the preceding rectangular forms (prostyle temples) or those surrounded by a single colonnade (peripteral temples) or sometimes a double colonnade (dipteral temples), the typical round temple developed, dating back to the extremely ancient form of the circular hut (Temple of Vesta, Temple of the Sibyl at Tivoli, Temple of the Boarian Forum).

At the highest point in the civilisation of the Empire, Hadrian, the emperor who was architect, poet and philosopher, decided to reunite, almost symbolically, the forms of Greek architecture and Roman architecture in the Pantheon, dedicated to all the gods. This was Rome's greatest temple; is also the only one to have come down to us intact and the only one in which Christianity was grafted directly onto pagan worship, so that as a temple it has remained alive throughout the centuries. From the functional point of view as well, the Pantheon transformed the concept of the temple which had prevailed until then: it was not a restricted chamber meant only to accommodate an image of the divinity and the priests, but an immense space which could contain a multitude of the faithful, no longer left outside as the " profane ". Indeed, it is a completely new concept, which foreshadows the Christian idea of *ecclesia,* the " church " conceived as the union of the faithful, formed in fact by the faithful themselves.

With respect to town-planning, the temples were the central points around which the streets, fora and monumental complexes developed, and we shall examine many of them in detail in our review of the monuments of ancient Rome.

ARA PACIS (ALTAR OF PEACE)

When Augustus returned victorious from his military campaigns in Gaul and Spain, he decided to celebrate the peace he had established with this monument: the *Ara Pacis Augustae* (Altar of Peace). Its construction was decreed in 14 B.C. and it was inaugurated in 9 A.D.

It is without doubt the monument which best qualifies the art of the Augustan age: the meeting-point between the refined elegance of the Hellenistic art of the East and the conscious grandeur of the Roman character. Apart from its artistic value, the Ara Pacis has a profound political significance, which is that of celebrating a will to create peace: the Roman peace of Augustus. It is peace elevated to the rank of divinity.

The monument consists of a quadrangular enclosure with two doors on the east and west sides, and in the centre is the altar. The internal walls of the enclosure are decorated with reliefs of garlands and bucrania (ox-skull motifs). The exterior, which is the more important part, has reliefs at the sides of the doors depicting the origins of Rome: the Lupercal, the sacrifice of Aenea, the personifications of the Earth and of Rome. On the lower part, around the four sides, there is an interlaced frieze with acanthus leaves and various small animals; on the upper part of the two long sides is shown a long procession led by Augustus.

Ara Pacis Augustae: relief panel showing the inaugural procession; in the middle, the figure of Agrippa.

PANTHEON

The Pantheon represents the highest expression of the Romans' genius as architects and builders.

Its origin dates back to Agrippa, who between 27 and 25 B.C. built a temple dedicated to all the gods, in order to create an ideal centre for the new area of the city in the Campus Martius. However, we cannot have any idea of the appearance of the Pantheon of Agrippa, because the temple was completely rebuilt in a different form between 120 and 125 A.D. by the emperor Hadrian. The latter, in an act of modesty even more marked when one considers that he himself must have conceived and supervised the construction of the new building, replaced word for word on the temple's façade Agrippa's original inscription.

The form of Hadrian's Pantheon is exceptional in every respect when compared with the other temples of ancient times: it consists in fact of two clearly distinct parts, a pronaos with columns and a gigantic circular chamber covered with a cupola, which completely dominates the whole structure.

The pronaos, in the traditional style of the Greek temples, consists of 16 monolithic columns, the eight on the façade of grey granite, the four on the sides and the four internal ones of pink granite, surmounted by splendid Corinthian capitals of white marble: each column is 41 feet high and weighs nearly 60 tons.

The pronaos is linked to the rotunda by means of a rectilinear structure, as wide as the portico itself and as high as the rotunda, decorated with large fluted " paraste " and with friezes, candelabra and festoons.

The architectural beauty of the Pantheon stands out above all in the interior, because of the perfect harmony of its proportions, because of the rhythm created by the alternation of structural elements and empty spaces and the subdivision into various levels, and because of the overall majesty of the building.

The secret of the proportions of the interior lies in the perfect equality of its diameter and height (141ft 9in), so that a perfect circle could theoretically be inscribed in the chamber and its upper half would constitute the inner curve of the cupola.

This is the largest existing cupola built in brickwork up to our time, 2ft 6in wider than St Peter's, 4ft 4in wider than that of the Cathedral of Florence and 49ft 4in wider than St Paul's in London.

The massive cylindrical wall which supports the cupola is lightened and given a sense of movement by eight large openings, two of them with arches for the entrance and the apse and six with architraves. On the front of these six openings and at the sides of the apse, the architrave is supported by splendid twin monolithic columns of old-gold and "pavonazzetto" marble. The floor retains, despite much restoration, the design and quality of the marbles (among which the porphyry stands out) used in the original paving.

The decoration of the attic, with its false windows, is the result of a cold and incorrect work of restoration done in the 18th century; only a small part on the right has been reconstructed according to its original appearance, with pilaster strips of porphyry imitating a colonnade which must have given the impression of supporting the cupola.

The cupola (of which Dion Cassius wrote that it resembled the vault of the sky) is also lightened by five concentric orders of lacunars, not added to the structure but created by casting, culminating in the great eye at the summit, almost 30 feet wide, which illuminates the whole interior.

This single source of light, coming from above, is of great importance in the overall effect of space in the building, since the illumination is thus uniform and devoid of strong contrasts.

Just as admirable as its architectural harmony is the construction technique used in building the Pantheon, a masterpiece in the use of cement work which, along with the considerable use made of the arch and the vault, was the greatest and most lasting achievement of Roman engineering.

The covering of this immense space (some 1,900,000 cubic feet) was achieved above all by the concentration of its weight and thrusts onto eight massive pillars of brickwork which are part of the supporting ring; and secondly by the use of horizontal layers of concrete containing different materials, becoming lighter towards the top (chips of travertine, of tufa, of brick and of volcanic scoriae),

◀ **Reconstruction model of the Pantheon area: in the centre of the square, the Arch of Piety.**

Interior of the Pantheon, first erected by Agrippa in the 1st century B.C., reconstructed in a different form by Hadrian in 123 A.D.

the thickness of which gradually diminishes from 19ft 4in at the base of the cupola to 4ft 11in at the summit.

The ring around the great eye serves as the keystone of the vault; it is made of brickwork 4ft 6in thick.

This massive concrete casting, which gives the whole building the solidity of a monolithic structure, is reinforced by a layer of brickwork on the cupola and by a layer of waterproof plaster 6 inches thick, formerly covered by bronze tiles.

The completion of the huge building must have taken more than a century, since Septimius Severus and Caracalla carried out restorations, recalled in an inscription on the architrave. It was one of the very few monuments which emerged unscathed from the destruction wrought by the barbarians, and with the advent of Christianity it became a church dedicated to Our Lady and all the martyrs, after the Byzantine emperor Phocas handed it over to Pope Boniface IV in 608.

The popes carried out many restorations of the Pantheon, especially Urban VIII and Alexander VII with the reconstruction of the left-hand corner of the pronaos where they replaced three fallen columns with others from the nearby Alexandrine Baths; but they also carried off much material.

Urban VIII (Barberini) himself removed the bronze covering of the pronaos for the casting of the baldachin of St. Peter's (" quod non fecerunt barbari, fecerunt Barberini " — what the barbarians left undone, the Barberini completed).

From the 16th century on, the Pantheon became the burial place for illustrious men, especially artists: Raphael and his beloved Maria da Bibiena, Annibale Caracci, Baldassarre Peruzzi, Perin del Vaga, Giovanni da Udine, Taddeo Zuccari, Vignola, Corelli.

Ever since the Renaissance, artists and scholars have expressed the greatest admiration for the Pantheon, which was taken as a model by Bramante, Raphael and Palladio; Michelangelo defined it as " not a human but an angelic design."

Again in the Baroque period Bernini (even though guilty of adding two ugly bell-towers to its façade, which were called " asses' ears " and demolished in 1882) found in the Pantheon inspiration for his masterpiece, the church of San Andrea al Quirinale, and during the neoclassical period its forms were reproduced innumerable times in many cities in Europe and America, including the Congress building in Buenos Aires and the Capitol building in Washington.

The name was also used for buildings in which the illustrious were to be buried, such as the Pantheon in Paris and the Pantheon of the Kings at the Escurial Palace in Madrid.

To conclude with the words of Roberto Vighi, from whose study we have drawn this careful description: " No other monument summarises in itself so much history and so much art, and no other has influenced the architecture of the whole world for so many centuries "

OBELISKS IN ROME

The obelisks were brought to Rome after Egypt became part of the Roman Empire. It was the emperor Augustus who had the great obelisk of Ramses II transported from Heliopolis towards 10 B.C., in order to place it on the spina in the centre of the Circus Maximus. Also brought from Heliopolis in the same period by order of Augustus was the obelisk of the 7th century B.C., now standing in front of Montecitorio, which the emperor had erected in the vicinity of the present-day site. The obelisk served as the "gnomon" or pointer of a large sun-dial.

Also from the time of Augustus are the two obelisks which stood at the sides of his Mausoleum, now on the Esquiline and on the fountain of the Quirinal.

The various obelisks in Piazza della Minerva, on the fountain in Piazza del Pantheon, at the Villa Albani, on the Dogali monument, in the Boboli Gardens in Florence and in the spheristerion at Urbino all come from the Temple of Isis which stood in the Campus Martius near the Temple of Hadrian.

The obelisk in front of Santa Trinità dei Monti comes from the Garden of Sallust, in the vicinity of the Porta Pinciana, where it still lay in 1557. It was erected on its present site in 1789.

The obelisk on the Fountain of the Rivers in Piazza Navona came from one of Domitian's villas near Albano. It was placed on the spina in the Circus of Maxentius, and was eventually incorporated by Bernini into his fountain in 1649.

The obelisk on the Pincian Hill comes from a monument erected in honour of Antinous on the Via Labicana. Transferred in 1633 to the courtyard of Palazzo Barberini, it was later moved to the Pigna courtyard in the Vatican, and Valadier moved it yet again in 1822 to the Pincio. The two latter obelisks belong to the Roman era, as the imitation hieroglyphics adorning them indicate.

The last of the great obelisks, the highest and the most ancient, that of the pharaohs Totmes II and IV (1500 B.C.), comes from Thebes. It was brought to Rome by Constantius II in 357 A.D. and erected on the spina of the Circus Maximus, making a pair along with that of Augustus.

Egyptian obelisk in Piazza della Minerva of the 6th century B.C., from the nearby Temple of Isis. The elephant on which it stands, designed by Bernini (1667), is jokingly called the "Minerva chick".

◀ **Egyptian obelisk in St. Peter's Square, originally on the spina of the Circus of Caligula-Nero (84 feet high).**

Hadrian's Villa - Private Library: full-size reconstruction in the Museum of Roman Civilization.

LIBRARIES AND SCHOOLS

The libraries of ancient Rome were built according to specific architectural principles. They were almost always composed of two rectangular areas thus separating the Latin from the Greek works. There was a large room with rectangular niches along the walls for the cupboards that held the books (scrolls, parchments and papyruses). Sometimes there were two or three levels of niches above each other. Around the main hall were smaller rooms which were used as library offices. Often the library had a portico where those who used the building could meet and converse. Around the inside walls ran a ledge and on the walls were portraits of famous authors and philosophers and on the back wall there was a larger niche that held a statue of Minerva.

Libraries were often a part of a larger architectural complex particularly baths and temples; there was a library in the Baths of Caracalla and in the temples of Apollo Palatinus, of Augustus, of Peace and even perhaps in the Pantheon.

The first library was that of Asinius Polio (28 B. C.) and was situated in the Atrium Libertatis. There was another in the Imperial Palace of Tiberius and also the famous ones symmetrically flanking the Emperor's column in Trajan's Forum.

At the end of the Empire it is estimated that Rome had about 40 public and hundreds of private libraries. The organisation of these libraries was very similar to todays; in fact it was possible for the libraries users to borrow books and to consult them at their leisure. Lanciani cites the example of Aulus Gellius who, as a guest in a villa at Tivoli, ran to the public library to fetch a book by Aristotle to prove to his friends that iced water taken in the hot season caused serious upsets.

Books, or rather scrolls and papyruses, were extremely expensive. Cicero tells us that the average price of a book was about a million lire at todays rate, about a thousand dollars. This accounts for the large number of public libraries that were taken over by the State from the time of Augustus.

The most important area for book-selling in ancient Rome was the Argiletum (which lay between the Roman Forum and Suburra). Here the book-sellers and their copiers, the scribes, had elegant and well stocked shops. They are aften mentioned and described in Martial and Horace.

Alongside the entrance of each shop was the striking publicity with titles and prices of the new books on sale. Each book-seller, or rather publisher, specialised in a particular author. Thus the Sosius brothers marketed Horace; Atrectus and Secundus, Martial; Quintus Atticus, Cicero; Dorus, Seneca and Tryphon, Quintilian.

Though it might seem incredible for those times the scribes were able to make up to 100,000 copies of each work and release them simultaneously in various centres of distribution (Pliny the Younger). Despite the fabulous profits of the publishers, given the price of books, the authors received no royalties but only random payments.

There were no special school buildings and teaching took place in certain parts of the Forums and the basilicas.

There was a school in the Basilica Argentaria, in Caesar's Forum, where the students left graffiti in the form of letters and lines from Virgil etc. In the 4th century A.D. there were also schools in the Forum of Augustus and in the hemicycle of Trajan's Forum. The Athenaeum, the "ludus ingenuarum artium", was probably the first purpose built university and was founded by Hadrian.

TRIUMPHAL ARCHES

The triumphal arch is generally held to be a creation of the Romans. It should be remembered that the triumphal arches were erected to fulfil a functional and harmonious role in Rome's town-planning, becoming an integral part of the city. They were often built to span a road (Arch of Titus on the summit of the Via Sacra) or to serve as entrances to monumental zones (Arch of Trajan at the entrance to the forum of the same name). Sometimes, too, they were built as a base for statues. The oldest arches of which there is mention in Rome are the barrel-vaults of L. Sertinius in the Boarian Forum and in the Circus Maximus, dating from 196 B.C., on which there were statues of gilt bronze. The next to be built was the Arch of Scipio on the Campidoglio (190 B.C.) From the regional catalogues, we know of the existence of 36 triumphal arches. Even though most of them have been destroyed, those which survive are more than enough to allow us to evaluate their aesthetic and architectural importance as an element of the town-planning and as a symbol of the art and history of ancient Rome.

Arch of Titus

The Arch of Titus, the monumental entrance to the Roman Forum at the highest point on the Via Sacra, was erected to celebrate the triumph of the Emperor over Judaea, conquered in 70 A.D. The splendid dedicatory inscription on the attic dates its construction as belonging to the time of Domitian (81-96 A.D.), after the death of Titus, who in the inscription is called *divus* (a title conferred by the Senate only on emperors who had been worthy of it during their lifetimes). The arch's simplicity and the nobility of its proportions and sculptural decorations make it a fine example of sobriety and equilibrium.

The reliefs on the inside of the arch represent the two principal scenes in the triumphal procession. On one side are depicted the soldiers bearing the spoils taken from the Temple of Jerusalem, the seven-branched candelabrum, the silver trumpets and the table for the bread, along with the two plaques on which the names of the conquered cities of Judaea were to appear.

The procession is about to pass under an arch, only half of which appears because the other half was painted. In fact, it should be remembered that the relief was a polychrome work. In the other relief can be seen the chariot of the Emperor, with the legionaries crowded around it: the Goddess of Victory is in the act of crowning the Emperor and the Goddess Rome, dressed as an Amazon, holds the bridle of the horses.

Even though they have reached us in a deplorable state of preservation, the reliefs from the Arch of Titus are considered the highest expression of the illusionist style of sculpture.

Arch of Titus, on the Via Sacra, erected by Domitian at the end of the 1st century A.D. in honour of the Divus Titus to celebrate the Roman conquest of Judaea. It was restored by Valadier in 1821.

The different depths of the relief-work and the contrasts of light and shade give the impression that the figures really move, and this effect must have been even greater when the colours and the gilding were still intact.

The two reliefs in the archway of the Arch of Titus, showing scenes from the Judaean triumph: above, the spoils of war borne in triumph; below, the chariot of the emperor.

Arch of Septimius Severus (203 A.D.)

This arch was built by Septimius Severus and dedicated to his sons Caracalla and Geta; later the name of Geta was removed by his brother Caracalla ("damnatio memoriae", the Roman process of eliminating all trace of a person's existence). The arch was erected to commemorate the first ten years of the Emperor's rule and to recall his victories against the Parthians, the Arabs and the people of Mesopotamia.

The arch has three barrel-vaults and the columns stand separate from the walls; originally the road did not pass beneath the vaults, this area being occupied by steps instead. On the attic, above the great inscription, there were statues of barbarians. Although the fine architectural proportions of the arch made it a model of its kind, the excessive sculptural decorations detract from this; these decorations include scenes from the Emperor's military campaigns in the East and the homage of the conquered peoples.

Arch of Septimius Severus (203 A.D.): side facing the Forum.

The Arch of Constantine with the Palatine in the background. ▶

Arch of Constantine

The Arch of Constantine, dating from 316 A.D., was erected to celebrate the Emperor's "decennalia" and his victory over Maxentius at the Ponte Milvio (312 A.D.).

It is of the same architectural type as the Arch of Septimius Severus, but is a superior work. In fact, by the harmonious distribution of its proportions, the design of the attic, the central part of which is reserved for the honorary inscription, and the placing of its many and varied decorative elements, it avoids the sense of crowding which can be felt in the Arch of Septimius Severus. Many of the decorations come from structures built in previous ages: the eight medallions above the arch's smaller passageways belong to the time of Hadrian, while the eight reliefs on the long sides of the attic are from the time of Marcus Aurelius. The figures of barbarians on the architraves of the columns and the reliefs on the short sides of the attic and on the walls of the main vault are from the period of Trajan. The friezes on the long and short sides belong to the era of Constantine and represent the Battle of Ponte Milvio, the siege of Verona or of Susa, and the Emperor's triumphal procession with his gifts to the people.

These reliefs done in Constantine's time are rendered in schematic form, creating a mass of inanimate figures; the figure of the Emperor himself has none of the dignified majesty of Marcus Aurelius or Trajan, and can only be distinguished from the others because of its greater dimensions.

The Arch of Constantine offers some extremely interesting and direct comparisons from the art historical point of view: in the great difference between the older sculpture and that of the 4th century should be seen, not so much a period of decadence for the figurative arts, but rather the birth of a new sort of art, closely bound to a new conception of life.

49

The four-fronted Arch of Janus (marking a crossroads) at the Velabrum; it dates back to the beginning of the 4th century A.D. and was probably dedicated to Constantine.

GARDENS AND VILLAS

Rome had numerous and magnificent gardens (horti) many of which in time became Imperial property and were often used as public parks.

Gardens were developed from the Ist century B.C. The favourite area was the Pincio which was called the *collis horticulorum*. Here the superb gardens of Alcilius Glabrius, the Anicius family and of Lucullus were situated. Between the Pincio and the Quirinal hills were the Gardens of Sallust, thought to be among the finest of ancient Rome and on the right bank of the Tiber were the Gardens of Lollia Paulina, of Mecenate, of Elio Laumia and of the Taurians.

The aim of the gardens was to achieve an harmonious fusion between architecture and nature. They were decorated with fountains, races courses, nymphaea and avenues with statues; often they were surrounded with a portico that made it possible to walk there both in the rain and in the heat.

The Romans used the term villa specifically to denote a residence outside the city which in its architectural layout took its inspiration from the *domus*, the city dwelling. Writers such as Cato, Varro, Vitruvius, Columella both give practical advice for the construction of villas and convery to us the love that their contemporaries had for country life which resulted from the agricultural origins of the Romans and the overpopulation of the city.

Villas and city residences with gardens often appear in Roman landscape painting in which the perspective shows the union of the residential quarters with garden, and the whole as a part of the surrounding countryside.

Villas were used in particular to house collections of art where the very rich gathered together sculpture, mosaics, books etc.

Villas were built both on the outskirts of the towns or directly outside the walls (the suburban villas) and in the hills and by the sea (the country villas). In the latter there was always a part set aside for the cultivation and preservation of agricultural products.

The garden was geometrical in its conception and very closely linked to the building. In the villas of the nobles they were extremely refined and had symmetrical avenues lined with beds of flowers and aromatic herbs, bushes pruned into the shapes of animals and statues. The whole was completed by the picturesque effect of the artificial use of water in small waterfalls, pools, canals, and in grottoes.

Among the many suburban villas we may mention that of the Quintilii on the Via Appia, of Gordianus at Tor de' Schiavi, the villa of Lucius Vero by the Acquatraversa bridge and the villa of the Sette Bassi on the Via Latina.

The architectural planning of the villas under the Empire followed Greek tastes, they become larger and freer in their design and aimed at a total union with nature. This is particularly apparent in the villas of the patricians and especially those of the Emperors where the imposing prospect of the central building was often adapted to the lay of the land. Such structural complexity is evident in the "Domus Aurea" which though it is located in the centre of Rome it may properly be regarded as a villa.

Domus Aurea: detail of the octagonal hall.

DOMUS AUREA

After the fire of 64 A.D. that destroyed a large part of Rome, Nero decided to replace his Domus Transitoria, which joined together the Emperor's property on the Palatine and the Esquiline, and began to construct the Domus Aurea on the Oppian Hill for which he expropriated 290 to 340 acres.

Tradition has passed down to us the name of two architects — Severus and Celere — who planned this incredible dwelling; it was more a villa than an urban imperial residence, combining simultaneously elements of the suburban ones and those found by the sea in Latium and Campania.

The façade was arranged in terraces on the slopes of the Esquiline Hill; it was an open colonnade that served as an entrance and ran along the Via Sacra.

Suetonius tells us that the circular dining room which, like the celestial spheres, turned constantly was one of its more incredible features; that the baths had both salt and sulphur waters and that the interior was decorated not only with stucco and painting but also with slabs of rare marble, ivory, precious stones and mother of pearl.

The most important innovation in the whole complex however was the octagonal hall which was over 42 feet wide and had a canopied ceiling with a circular opening in its centre. Rooms opened off five of its sides and the other three gave onto the terrace. The five radial rooms had barrel or cross vaulting and were decorated with niches. Here there are two features of extreme importance: the octagonal form that was to become typical of Roman architecture, and concrete was used in the vaulting, for the first time on a large scale.

The decoration of the interior was entrusted to Fabullus. He is mentioned by Pliny the Elder as a court painter in every respect. He painted for only a few hours each day and was always meticulously dressed, even on the scaffolding.

The decoration, for which Fabullus must have had many helpers, may be divided into two: that used in the corridors and that used in the rooms. In the corridors and in the barrel vaulting there were small landscapes, employing an impressionistic technique, done with small and rapid brush strokes which eliminated half tones and chairoscuro effects. This style was to be more fully developed in the catacombs and late antique painting. The landscapes alternated with walls painted to imitate wall-paper with little figures, flowers, candelabra and birds on a plain background. The walls of the rooms however were decorated with architectural painting which anticipated and excelled by a long way "the fourth Pompeian style"; it had a sophisticated use of space and placed the figures in different planes. The total effect was enhanced with gilding, semi-precious stones and sheets of ivory.

In the valley where the Colosseum now stands was an artificial lake with salt water; it was surrounded by buildings and on the slopes of the Coelian Hill was a huge nymphaeum with large niches.

HONORARY COLUMNS OF TRAJAN AND MARCUS AURELIUS

Column of Trajan

The Column of Trajan represents the triumph of the relief and of the sculptor's art in Rome. The touch of softness and smoothness which could still be seen in the sculpture from Nero to Domitian has been eliminated and the Hellenistic technique has been absorbed, so that in the relief on Trajan's Column the vigour of the figures is revealed and they are no longer idealised but made human and surrounded by the historical reality in which they moved.

The column has reached us almost intact, but the gilded statue of Trajan which stood on top of it has been lost and the ashes of the great ruler, contained in a golden urn placed in the base of the column, have been dispersed. The reliefs, although they are corroded, are intact: describing an upward spiral movement, they relate the exploits of the Dacian Wars (101-102; 105-107 A.D.). The spiral consists of 44 sections with a total length of some 650 feet.

There are no less than 155 scenes in which can be counted 2500 figures. The column stood in front of the Temple of Trajan and beside two libraries, one Greek and the other Latin.

The Column of Trajan between the two libraries of the Forum of Trajan: reconstruction (p. 53).

The Column of Trajan (113 A.D.), erected to celebrate the Roman conquest of Dacia (now Rumania). In the detail, scenes from Trajan's first campaign: loading provisions into the ships; religious ceremony; surrender of the barbarian chiefs to the Emperor.

Column of Marcus Aurelius

The Column of Marcus Aurelius was begun during the last years of the Emperor and completed under his son, Commodus. The present base is the work of Domenico Fontana, 1589.

The column was originally surmounted by the bronze group of Marcus Aurelius and Faustina, but now has a statue of St. Paul.

Here, as on Trajan's Column, the relief moves upwards in a spiral band; it celebrates the wars fought and the victories won by the Emperor against the Marcomanni, Quadi and Sarmathians between 171 and 175 A.D.

The Emperor is depicted 59 times, but in order to emphasise his gentle, philosophical nature he never appears either with sword in hand or in the scenes of battle.

Column of Marcus Aurelius, wrongly called Column of Antoninus (176 A.D.). At left, reconstruction of the area.

The epic, solemn tone of Trajan's Column is replaced in the Column of Marcus Aurelius by a more pictoric style and greater dramatic effects. The column rose in the middle of a monumental zone, rather like a new forum, in the Campus Martius. Alongside it was the " Ustrinum Antoninorum " where the bodies of the Imperial families were cremated.

In the same area once stood the Honorary Column of Antoninus Pius. Its base is now in the Belvedere niche in the Vatican.

Statue of Julius Caesar in Via dei Fori Imperiali (bronze casting of the marble statue in the Campidoglio).

Forum of Caesar, with the Temple of Venus Genetrix: reconstruction. ▶

THE IMPERIAL FORA

The Republican Forum had soon turned out to be insufficient to accommodate the political and administrative activities of the city which had in the meantime become the capital of an empire. Caesar, apart from reorganising the old Forum, reconstructed the Curia, changing its orientation; constructed the Basilica Julia, ordering the placing of the Rostra and the laying of the black marble paving called the Lapis Niger; and planned and began the construction of a new Forum nearby. In order to do this, it was necessary to expropriate an area occupied by private houses, and Caesar had to pay the fabulous sum of a million sesterces (several million pounds or dollars in our currency).

The Forum of Caesar

The Forum of Caesar was approved in 54 B.C. It had the form of an elongated rectangle (175 by 80 yards), and was surrounded by porticoes with booths. On the short side in front of the entrance stood the temple dedicated to Venus Genetrix. Almost square in form, this was an octastyle Corinthian temple, with a splendid lacunar ceiling. In the apse of the temple was the statue of the goddess by Archesilaus, a Greek sculptor of the neo-Attic school. There were also two statues of Caesar and one of Cleopatra.

Access to the temple was by stairs on the sides. The portico of the temple contained a rich collection of pictures by the most illustrious Greek painters, acquired or simply carried off by Caesar to adorn his Forum. Pliny mentions numerous works, among them one of Medea as she meditates the killing of her children and a portrait of Cleopatra. Also kept here were six chests of gems and a suit of armour made of precious metal. In front of the temple was a splendid fountain decorated with statues of nymphs by the neo-Attic school. Later, at the time of Trajan, the Basilica Argentaria was added, and the whole Forum underwent extensive restorations at the hands of Domitian, Trajan and Hadrian.

The Forum of Augustus

Augustus continued the town-planning policy of Caesar, expropriating private houses between the Suburra zone and the Forum of Caesar, and here in 42 B.C. he began work on his Forum and on the Temple of Mars Ultor (Mars the Vindicator), as the emperor himself records in his autobiography. The works were paid for with the proceeds of war booty. The square of the Forum was rectangular in form (135 by 98 yards) and at the sides were two covered hemicycles, semispherical structures 100 feet high, with Corinthian columns and caryatids. Work continued on the Forum for many years and when it was inaugurated in 2 B.C. it was still uncompleted; in fact, work continued for more than a century. In 19 A.D. Tiberius erected two arches in honour of

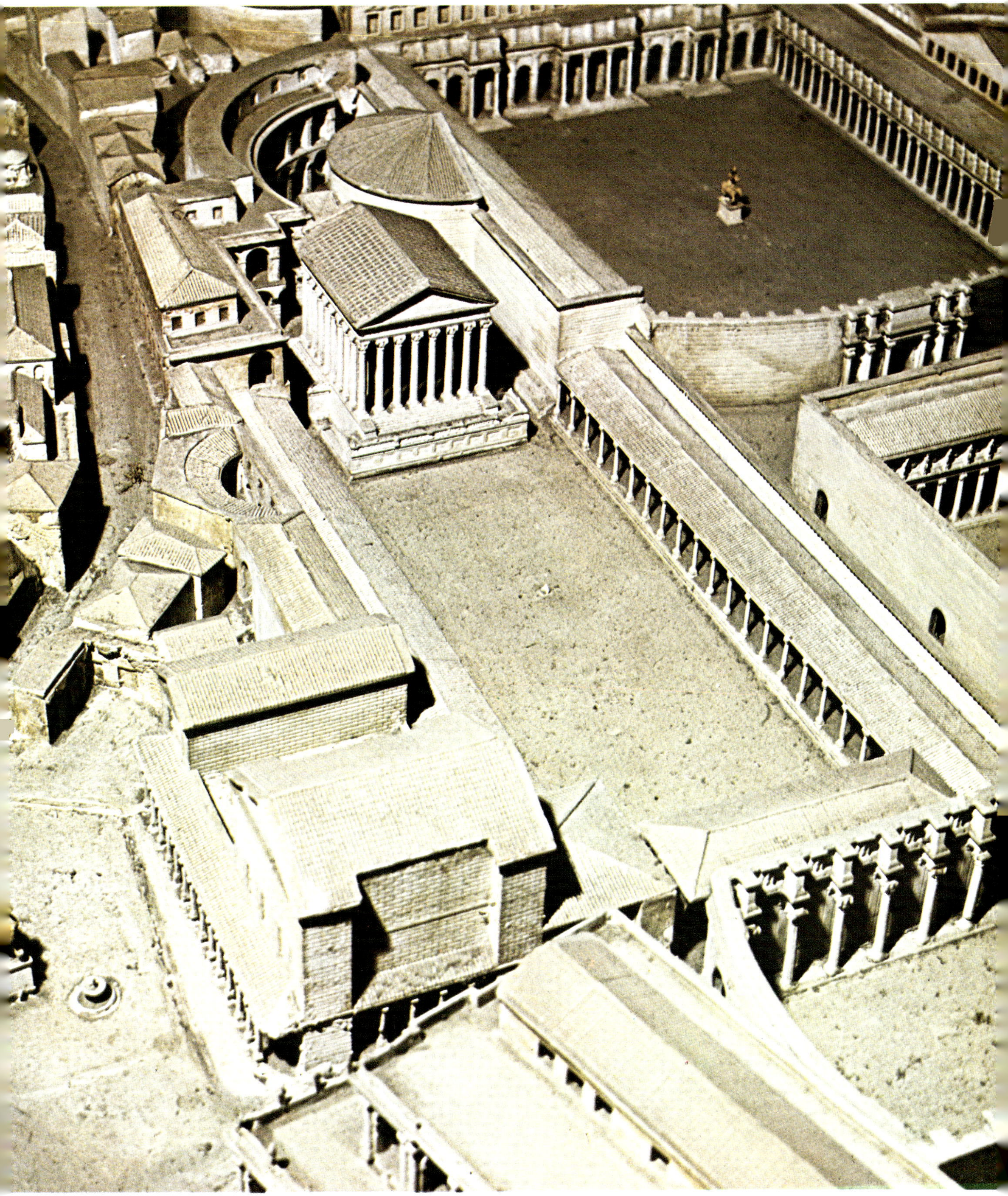

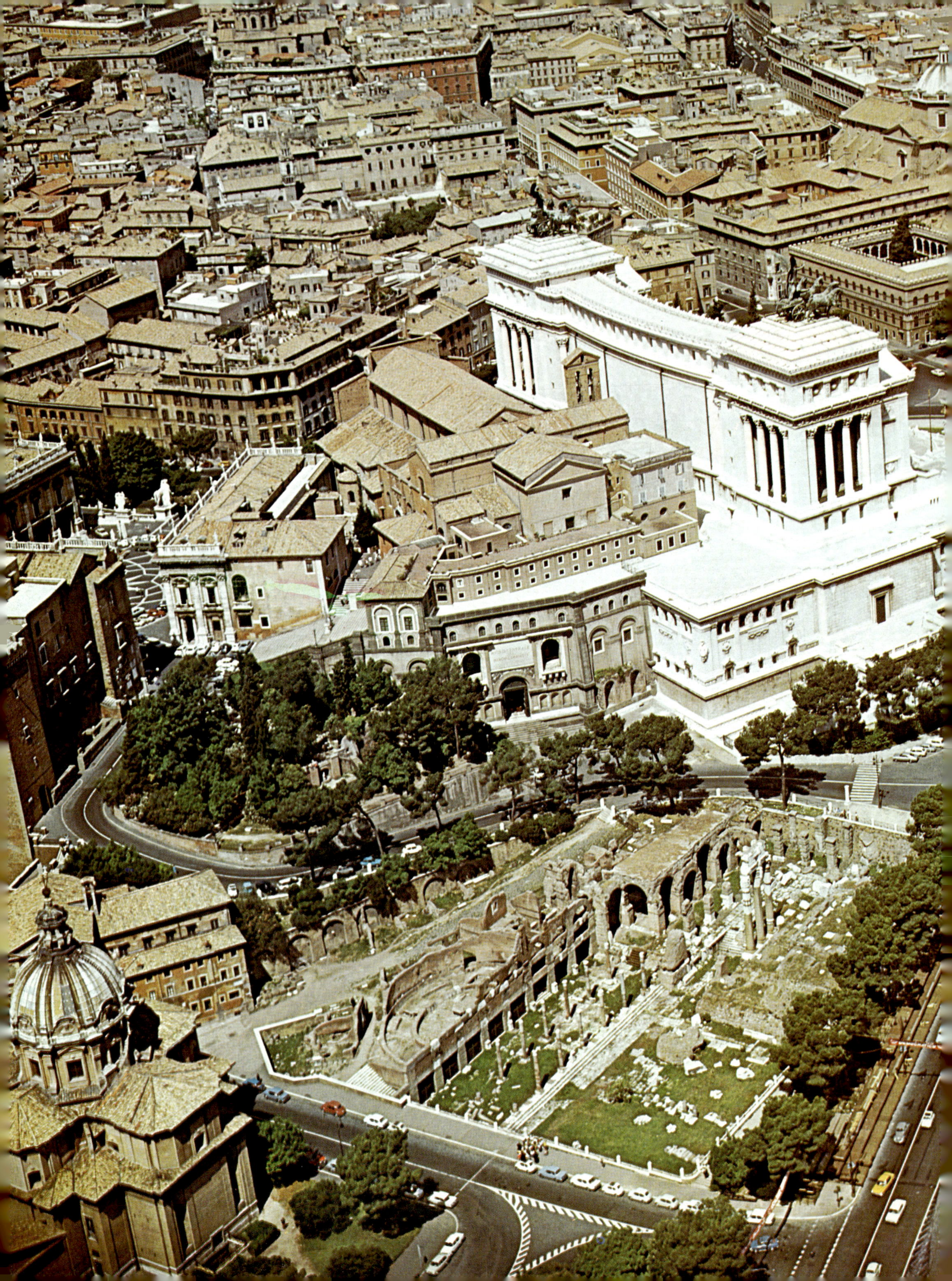

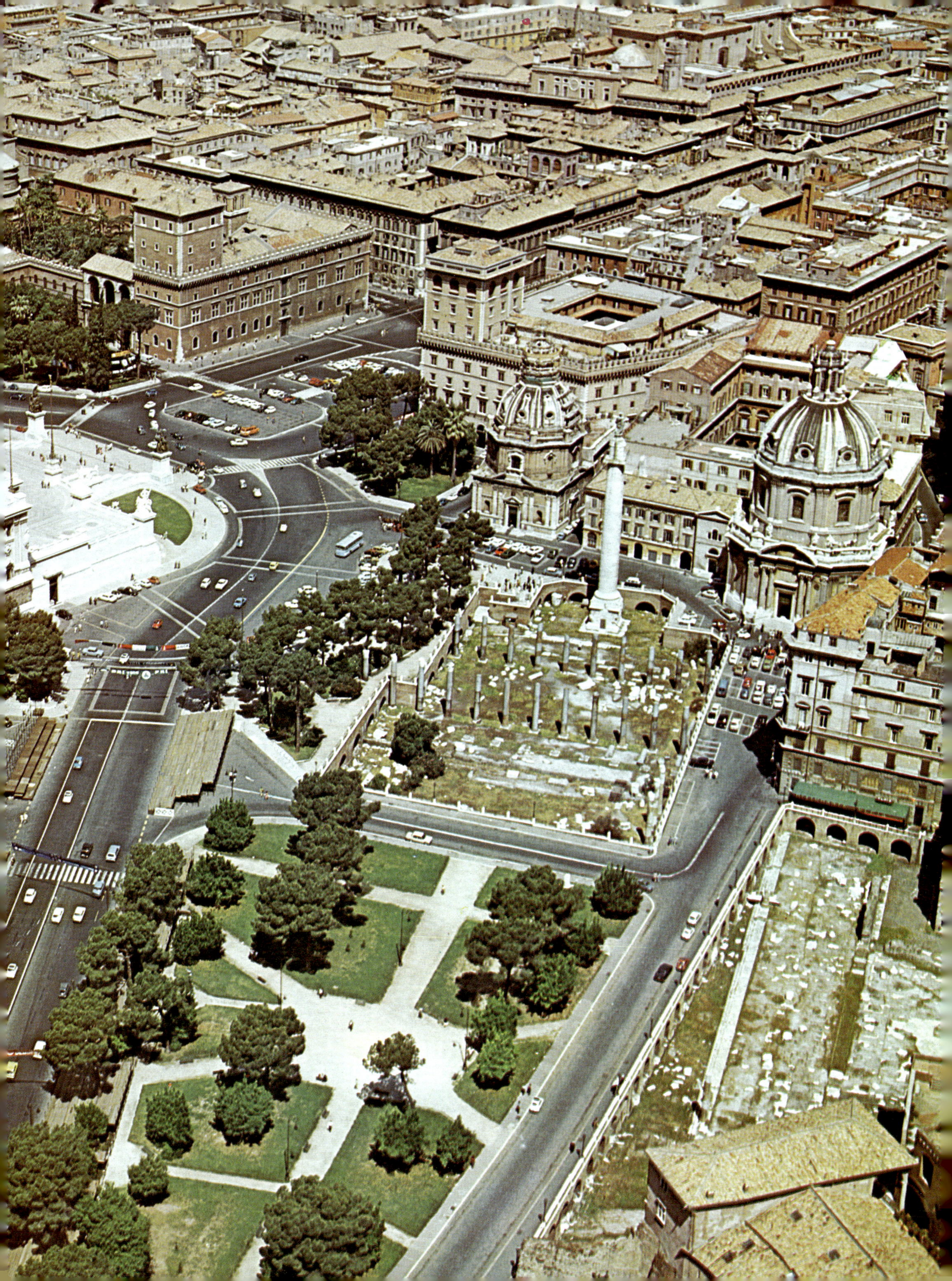

◀ Aerial view with the Campus Martius (top), the Campidoglic (centre), the Forum of Caesar (bottom left) and the Forum of Trajan (bottom right).

Drusus and Germanicus. Hadrian also made improvements and carried out restorations to the Forum which contained innumerable works of art, among them an ivory statue of Apollo and a bronze four-horse chariot dedicated to Augustus by the Senate. Augustus had statues of Rome's most illustrious military leaders, from Aeneas to those of his own time, placed in the hemicycles, and each statue had a eulogistic plate attached. The statue of Caesar stood out above all, and in the temple Caesar's sword was kept and revered as an important relic. According to Dion Cassius, the statues were of bronze, but the Historia Augusta says that they were marble. Probably they were partly of one and partly of the other material.

The Temple of Mars Ultor was constructed according to the Italic type: peripteral (with a single row of columns) on three sides, with a total of eight Corinthian columns on each side, built on a podium about 11ft 8in high and covered with marble, and with steps in front of the façade and the altar for sacrifices in the middle of the steps. In the apse stood the statues of Mars and Venus. At the side of the temple was the hall of the Colossus (giant statue) of Augustus, and on the walls, which were covered with old-gold, " pavonazzetto " and African marble, must have been the four paintings mentioned by Pliny, of which two were by the legendary Apelles.

In order to protect these splendid and priceless works of art from the frequent fires which broke out in the adjacent working-class area of Suburra, and also perhaps to hide that area's ugliness, Augustus had a wall of fireproof material (peperino and stone from Gabii) erected around the Forum.

Statue of Augustus in Via dei Fori Imperiali (bronze casting of the marble original in the Vatican Museum).

Forum of Augustus with the Temple of Mars Ultor: as it is today and reconstruction. ▶

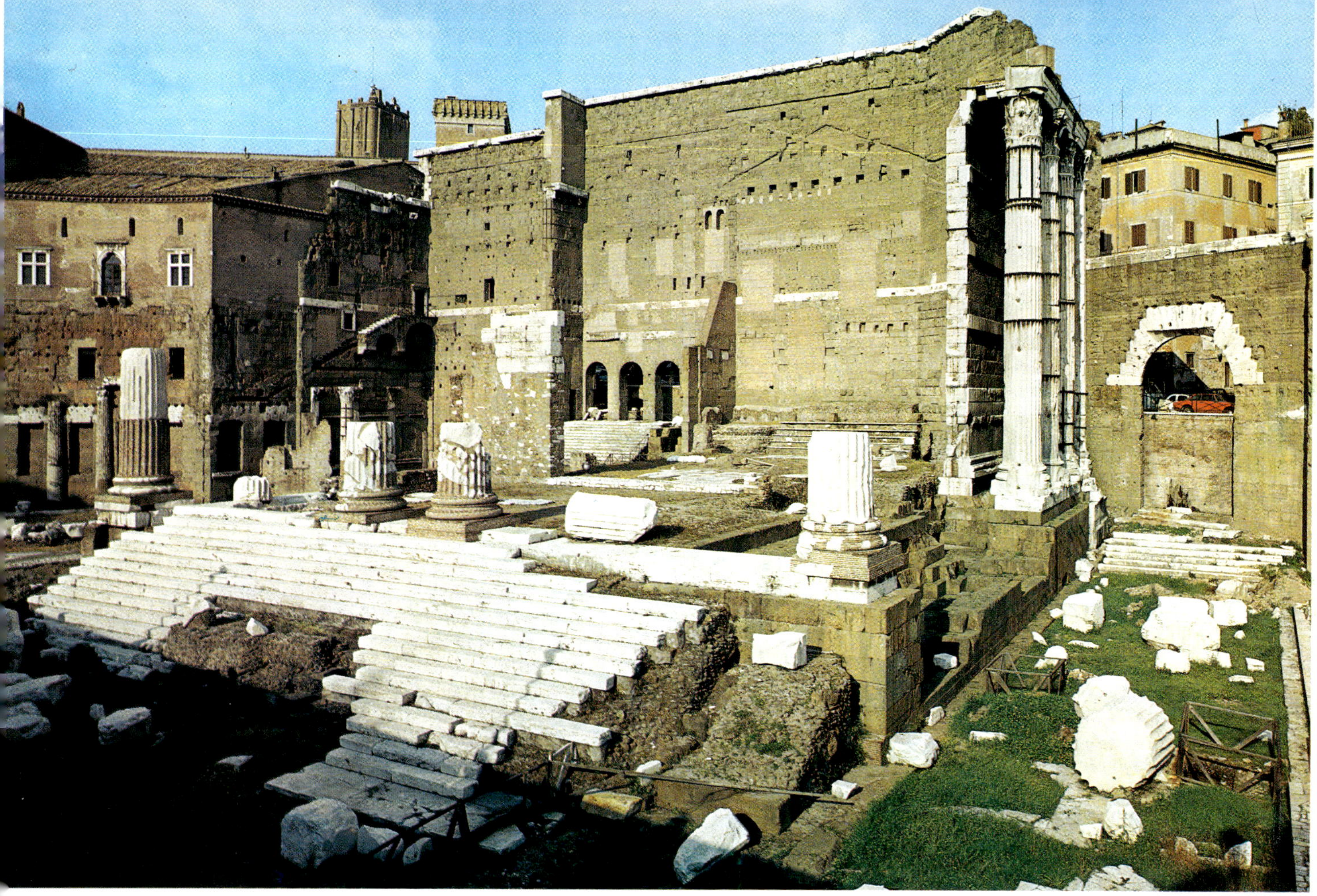

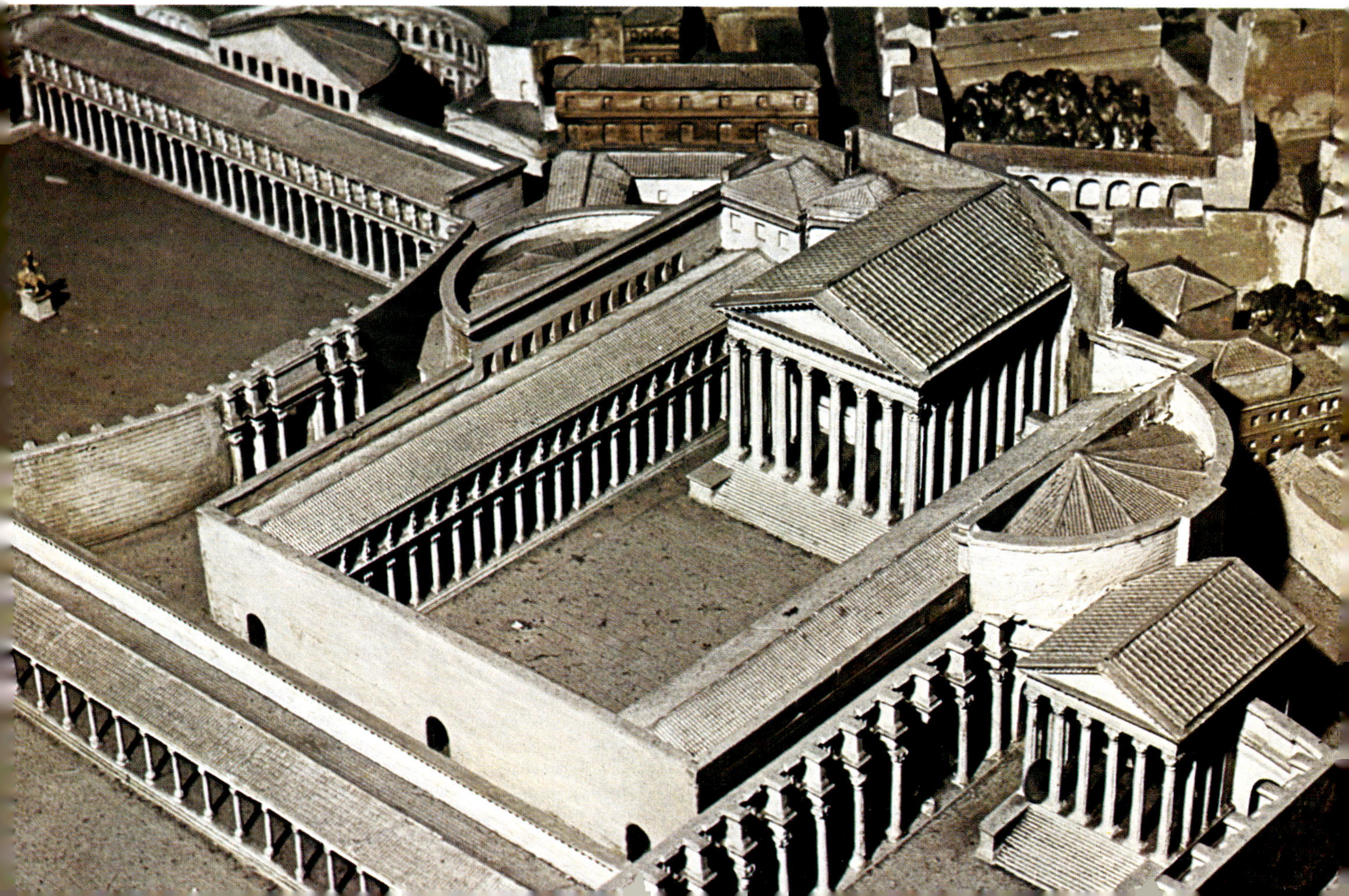

Forum of Vespasian with the Temple of Peace: reconstruction (end of 1st century A.D.).

The Forum of Peace

The third of the Imperial Fora was the Forum of Peace erected by the Flavian emperors; it was a large, porticoed square, in which stood the Temple of Peace, sometimes called of Vespasian. Of this entire monumental complex, which occupied the area between the present-day Via Cavour and the Colosseum, nothing remains; we know only that in the temple, as if in a museum, were kept the treasures carried off from Jerusalem, along with many works of art.

The Forum of Nerva

The Forum of Nerva was begun by Domitian and completed by Nerva in 97 A.D.; it was called the " Transitory " Forum, because through it passed the Via dell'Argileto linking the Forum with the Quirinal.

The temple was an octastyle Corinthian structure, dedicated to Minerva. In 1606 it was demolished by Pope Paul V, and its marble was used to construct the fountain on the Janiculum and the Borghese Chapel in the Basilica of Santa Maria Maggiore.

Statue of Nerva in Via dei Fori Imperiali: bronze casting.

Forum of Nerva with the Temple of Minerva: reconstruction (96-98 A.D.), with at left the Forum of Augustus and Temple of Mars Ultor.

The Forum of Trajan

The Forum of Trajan was the most splendid of all. The way for its construction had perhaps already been prepared by Domitian, who had begun to excavate the ridge on the Quirinal Hill, a work of considerable magnitude because the ridge was about 100 feet high. The final plan for the Forum was done by Trajan's great architect, Apollodorus of Damascus.

In order to avoid the danger of landslides, the markets were built with a series of large step-shaped structures which both solved the problem of stability and created an aesthetic solution for the whole complex.

The overall architectural complex consisted of a vast square with porticoes and two exedrae, which was entered from the Forum of Augustus through

Forum of Nerva or "Transitory" Forum: detail of the colonnade, called the "Colonnacce".

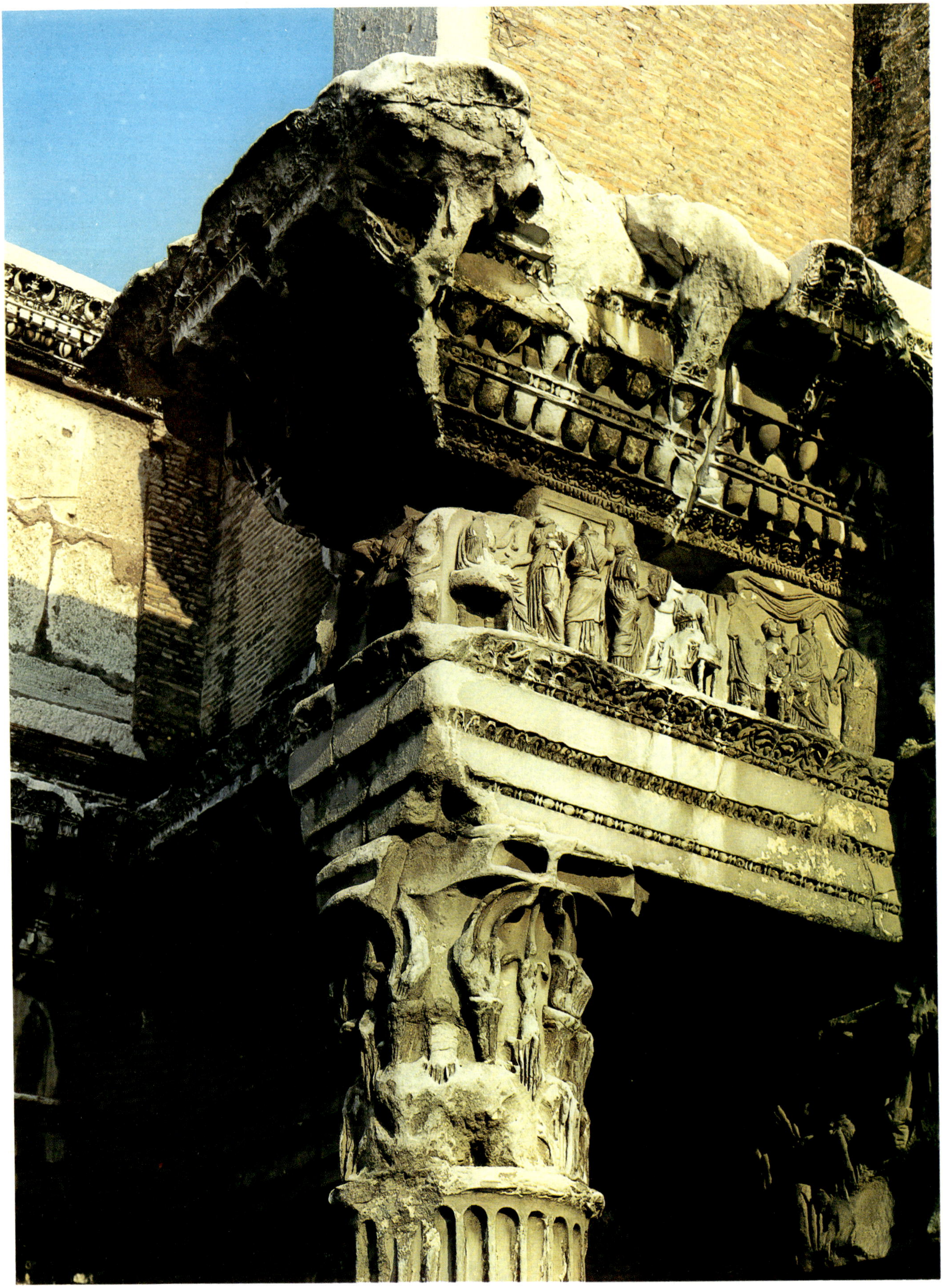

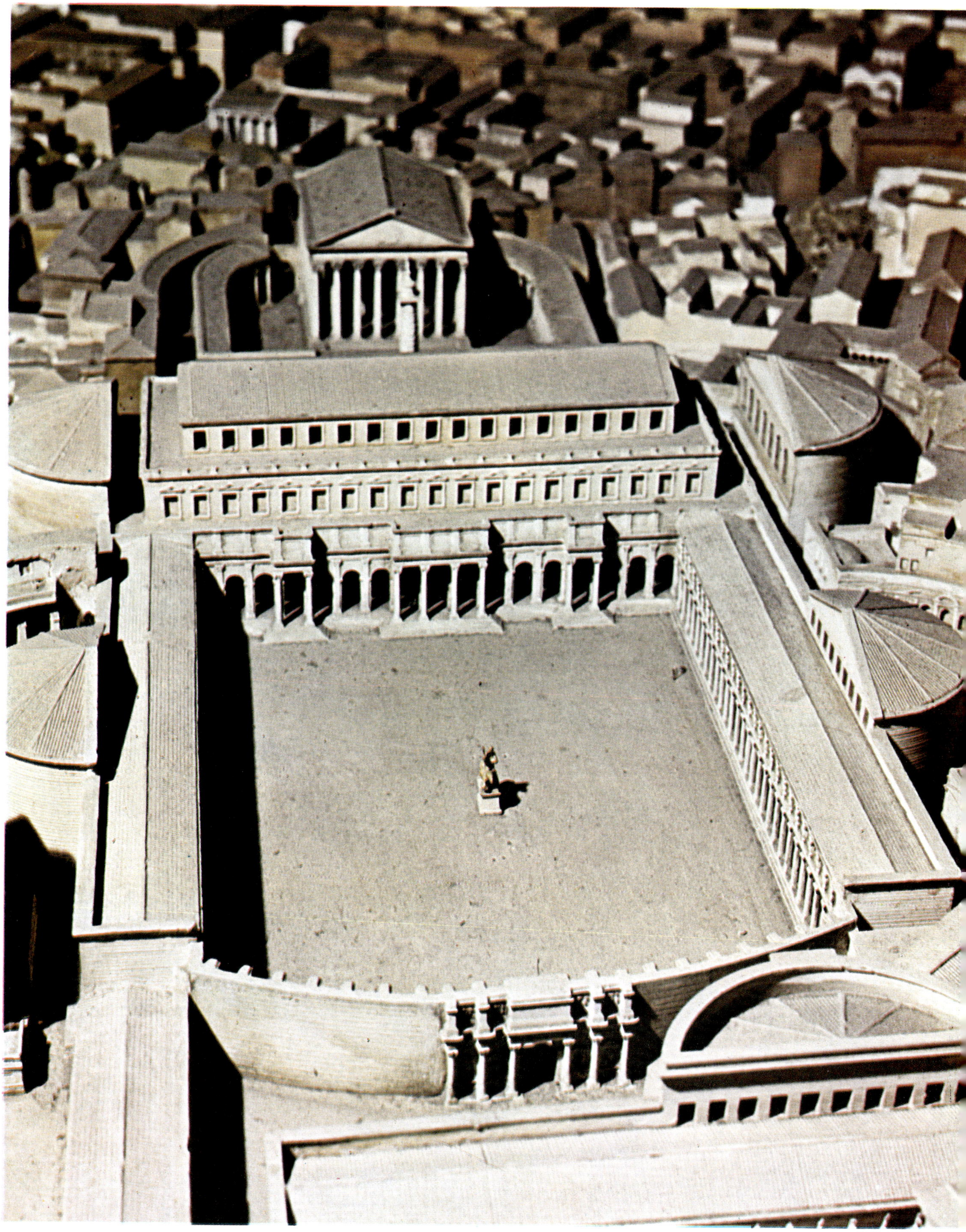

The Markets of Trajan, commercial centre of ancient Rome. Below, the large exedra with three levels of shops, following the lines of the enclosed square of the Forum of Trajan; higher up, another series of shops and stores, again in three levels, along Via Biberatica and in the large hall of Largo Magnanapoli. In the Markets of Trajan, apart from the usual commercial life, the distribution of foodstuffs to the people took place.

◀ Forum of Trajan, the work of Apollodorus of Damascus (beginning of the 2nd century A.D.): reconstruction.

a triumphal arch dedicated to Trajan. Facing the square, in the centre of which was the equestrian monument to the emperor, was the Basilica Ulpia, the largest in Rome, with nave, four aisles and two apses; its dimensions may be compared to those of the Basilica of San Paolo. Besides the Basilica Ulpia, there were two library buildings, Greek and Latin, between which stood the great Column of Trajan, with its reliefs commemorating the Roman conquest of Dacia (now Rumania). Further on again, the colossal Temple of Trajan must have stood, erected by his successor: it has completely disappeared, to make way for the construction of two churches, the Palazzo Valentini (now the Prefettura) and other buildings, among them the house of Michelangelo; nothing remains now except a column and a capital to remind us of its gigantic proportions.

COLOSSEUM

The Flavian Amphitheatre (this is the Colosseum's real name) was begun in the year 72 A.D. under Vespasian and inaugurated by the Emperor Titus in the year 80. The inauguration was a solemn event marked by 100 days of festivities. The writer Dion Cassius relates that during these festivities 9000 wild beasts were killed and some 2000 gladiators lost their lives.

The amphitheatre was completed, however, by the Emperor Domitian.

The amphitheatre consists of four floors. The first three are built with arches and adorned by half-columns of the Doric, Ionic and Corinthian orders respectively; the top floor has rectangular windows instead of arches and is decorated with pilasters with Corinthian capitals.

The first floor is 34ft 5in high and the Doric arches are 23ft 4in high and 14ft 0in wide.

The second floor, in the Ionic order, is 38ft 8in high and the arches measure 14ft 0in in width and 21ft 4in in height.

The third floor, in the Corinthian order, is 37ft 10in high and its arches are 21ft 0in high and 14ft 0in wide.

The Corinthian pilasters on the top floor are 45ft 6in high including the pedestal.

On each of the three levels with arches there were eighty passageways; those on the first level were numbered, except for the ones which corresponded to the structure's major and minor axes; the first two of these were the main entrances to the arena and the second two the entrances of the Emperors.

The numbers served to indicate which was the entrance most conveniently located for reaching the seating area allocated to the spectator according to his relative social rank.

For the external part of the amphitheatre and for much of the interior, the material used is travertine stone. The blocks were not held together with mortar but with pins of iron and other metals.

Reconstruction of the Colosseum area. From left: Temple of Venus and Rome, Colossus of Nero, Meta Sudans Fountain, Arch of Constantine, Colosseum, Baths of Titus; bottom right, two "Ludi gladiatorii", or gladiators' schools.

Flavian Amphitheatre or Colosseum (72-80 A.D.): reconstruction of the exterior.

The arena of the amphitheatre is 86 yards long and 50 yards wide. Around the arena there was a net to protect the spectators.

The surface of the arena, which consisted of wooden boards, was covered with sand, "arena" in Latin, which gives us the term still used today.

At the long ends of the arena there were two entrances: the south-eastern one was the "Libitinarian" gate (from Libitina, goddess of funerals), through which were carried the dead gladiators and the wild beasts which had been killed; the other was the entrance gate for the processions of gladiators who paraded before the Emperor and the spectators before the beginning of the combats. *Ave, Caesar, Morituri te salutant!* (Caesar, those about to die salute you!).

The subterranean areas beneath the arena served to contain everything that was necessary for the spectacles. There were cages to hold the wild beasts destined for the show and mechanical elevators by means of which the animals were made to appear on the surface of the arena. Also worth noting is the existence of no less than five cryptoportici (covered galleries or corridors), of which one was decorated with stuccoes, mosaics and paintings on the wall. This structure seems to have been added by the Emperor Commodus, who used it to pass directly into the amphitheatre.

The seating area began with a podium, and on two arms in the centre of this were the pulvinars or special cushioned seats: the one to the south-west was for the Emperors and the other one, opposite, was for the most important dignitaries and the Vestal Virgins. The pulvinars thus corresponded to the two main entrances; they were reached by way of two halls, each one divided by 18 travertine pillars with arcades decorated in stucco. The podium consisted of seven steps, with twelve entranceways or "vomitoria". Above the podium was a series of twelve steps limited by an 11ft passageway running all the way round. Its size is explained by the fact that there were forty dormer-windows which illuminated the portico, or ambulatory, below. This first section of the seating area had 14 entranceways and was reserved for the 14 orders of knights.

Above this there was another section of 19 steps, also limited by a parapet and a passageway. This section had 32 entranceways or " vomitoria ", and because it was very high it had 28 windows at the back to give light to the corridor behind it. Between the windows there were 36 niches containing statues. Above this was the top section, consisting of seven wooden seats, with the parapet forming the base of a portico with 80 columns; also at the base was the passage which had 12 entranceways.

From this outline, one can calculate the capacity of the amphitheatre, which must have held about 50,000 spectators, in any case not more than this.

To complete our general description, the velarium should be mentioned: this was a canopy which served to shelter the spectators from the burning sun. The velarium was hoisted on the terrace above the portico, and the operation was entrusted to the sailors from the Imperial Fleet of Misenum.

Interior of the Colosseum today, following the removal of the surface of the arena. ▶

The Colosseum seen from Via dei Fori Imperiali.

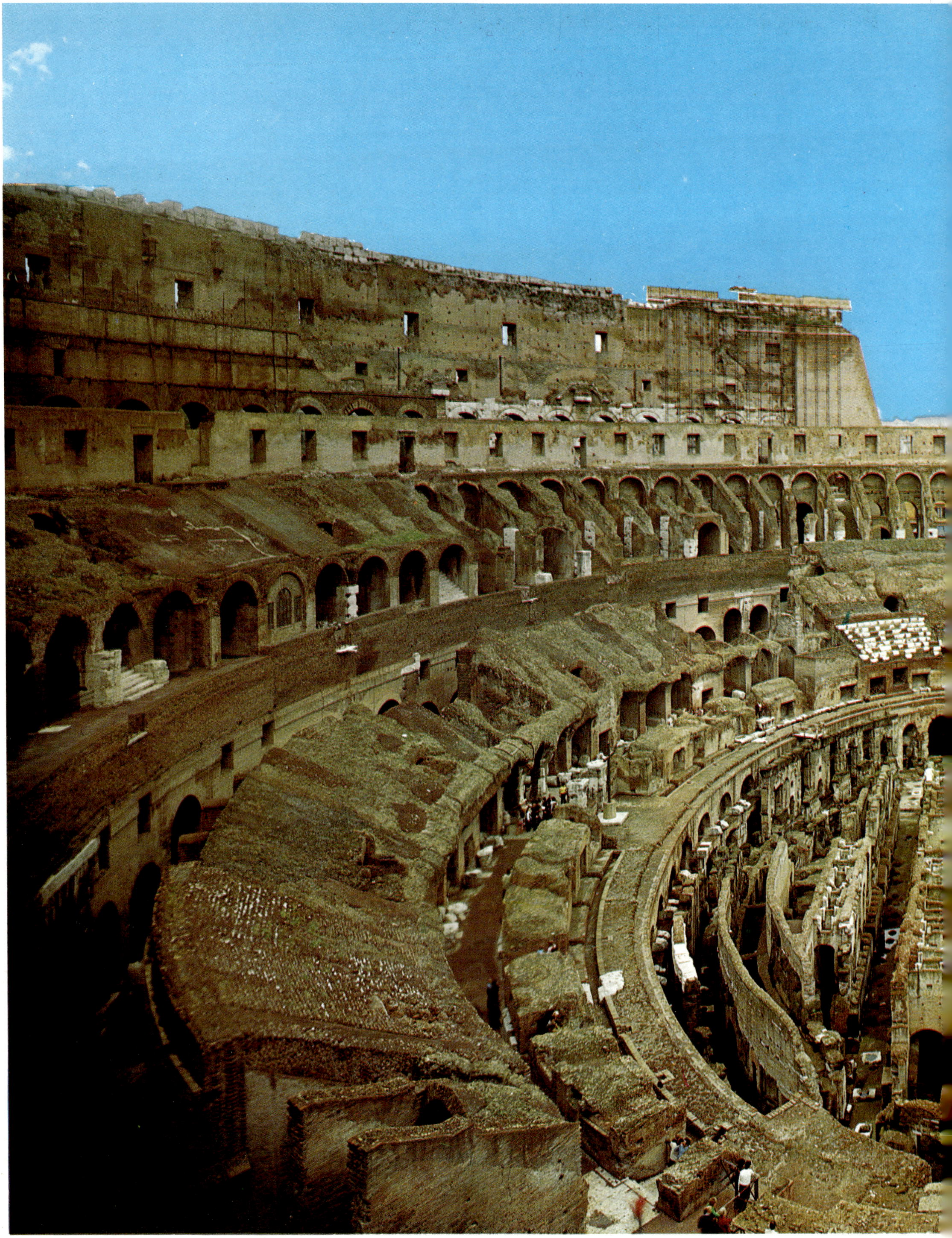

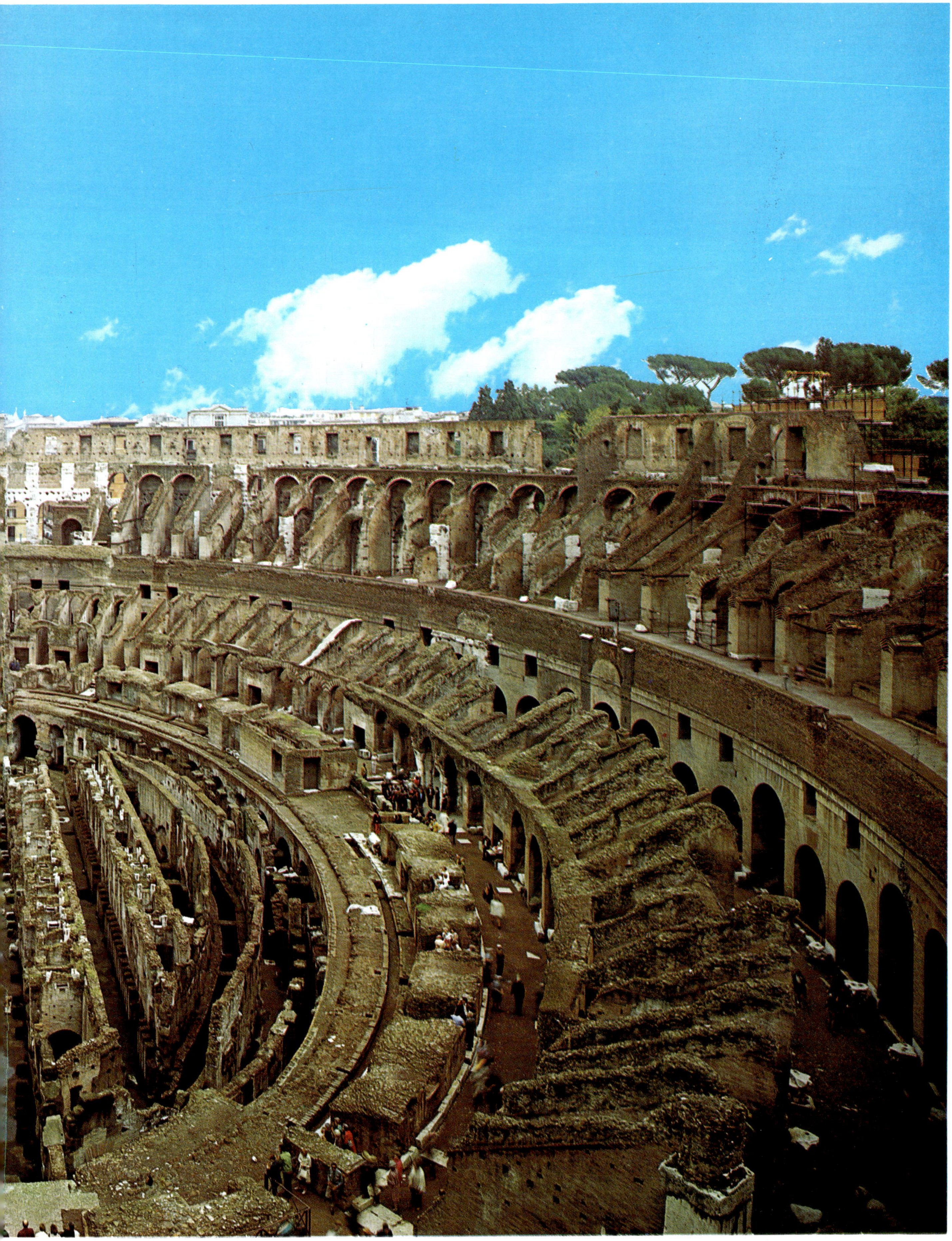

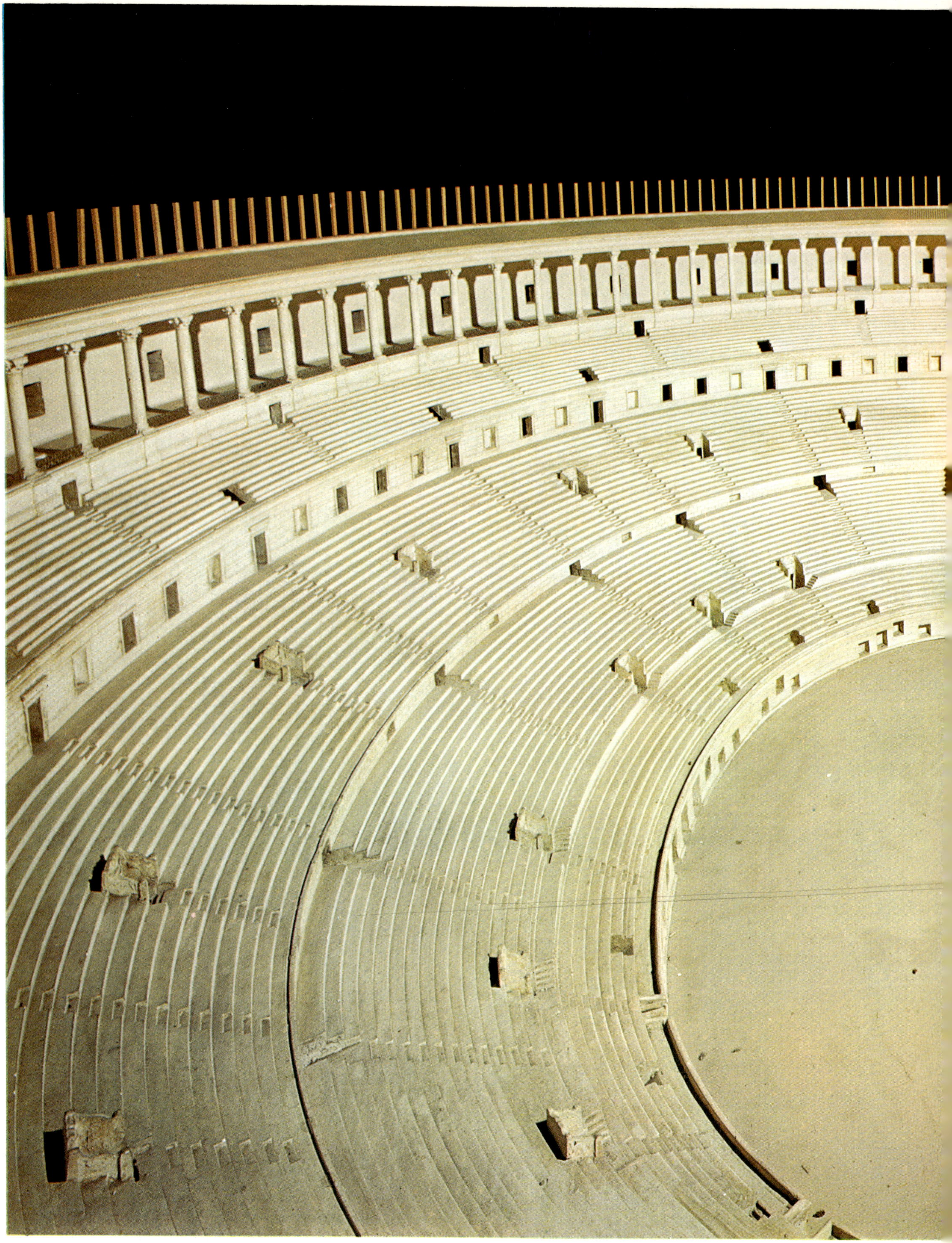

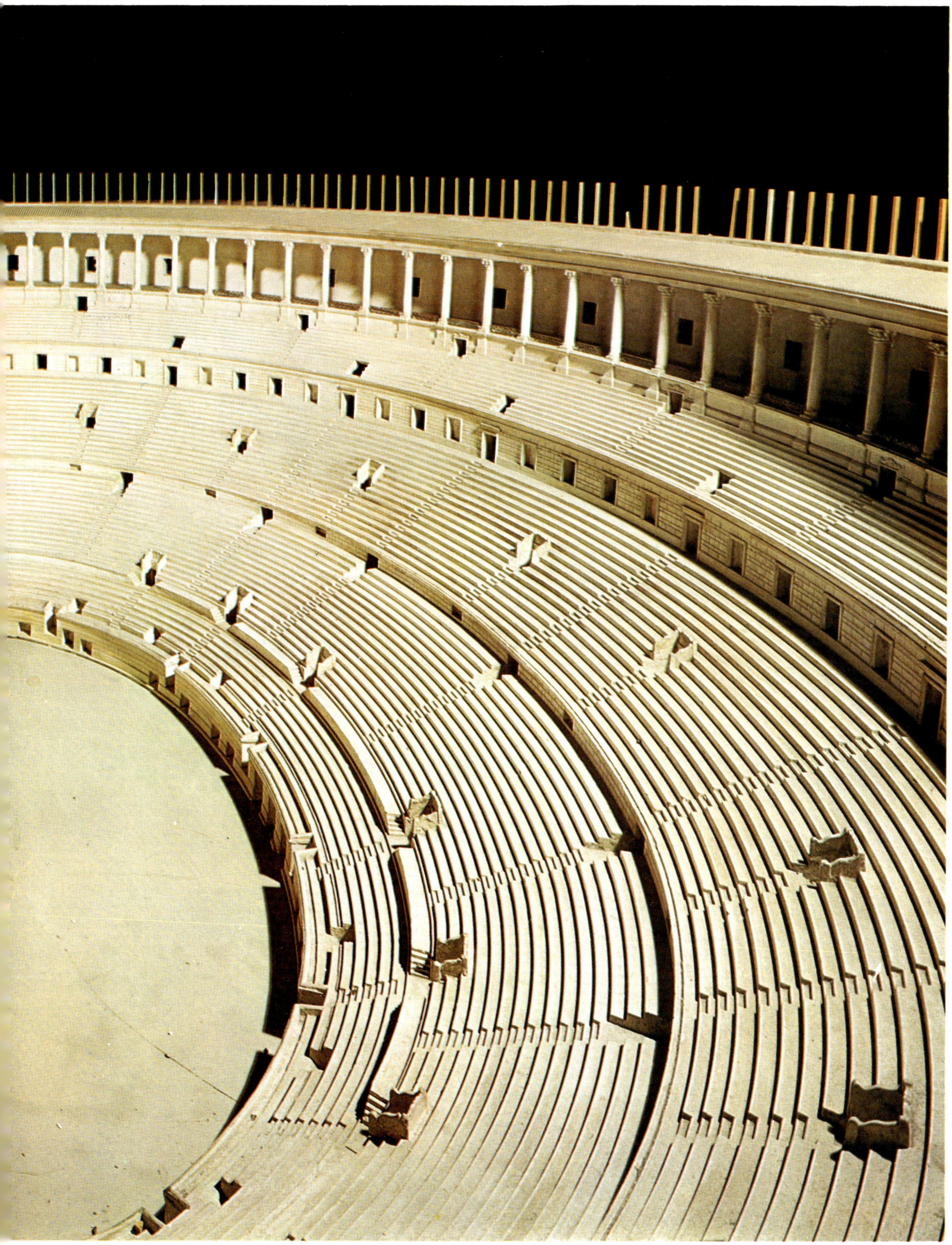

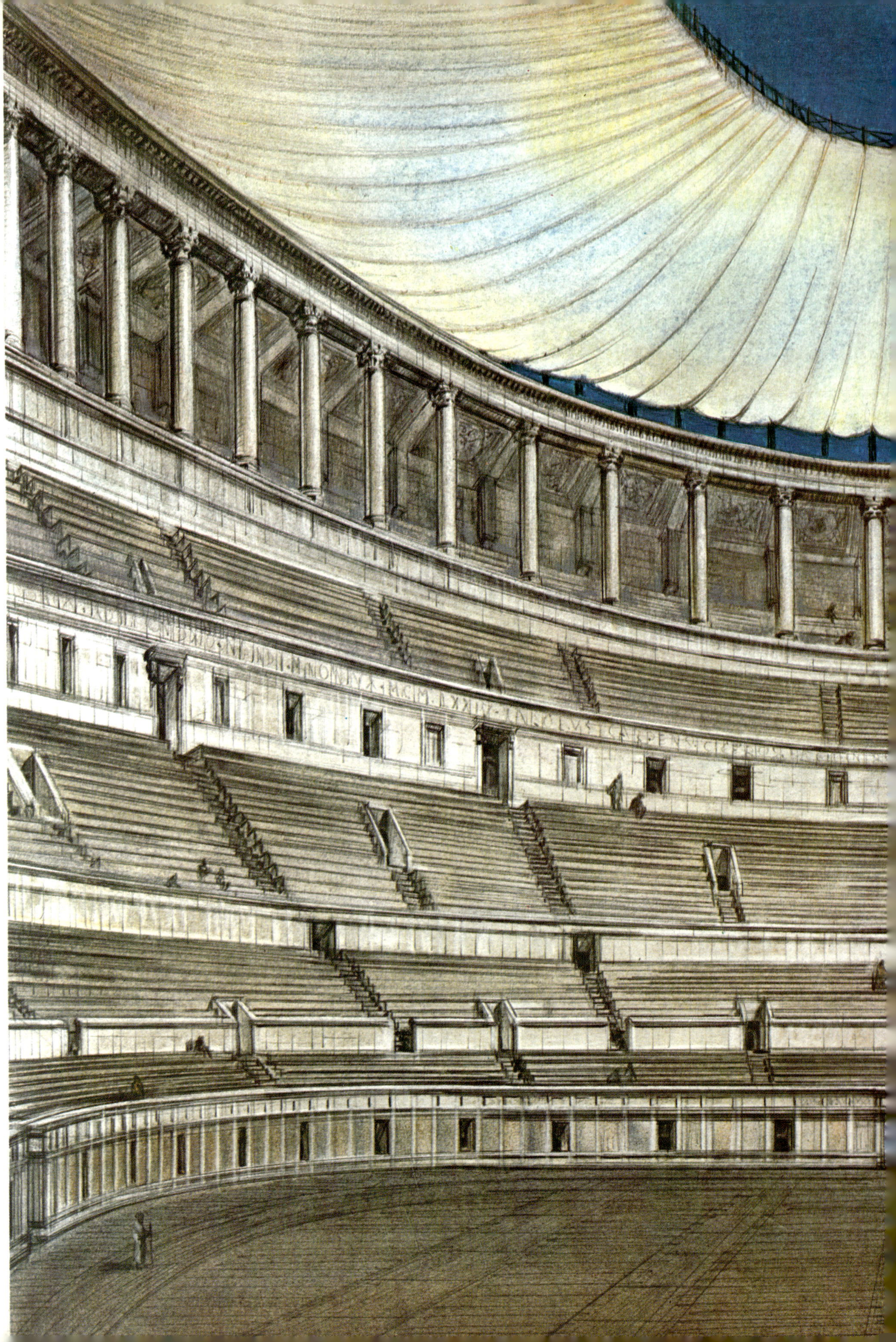

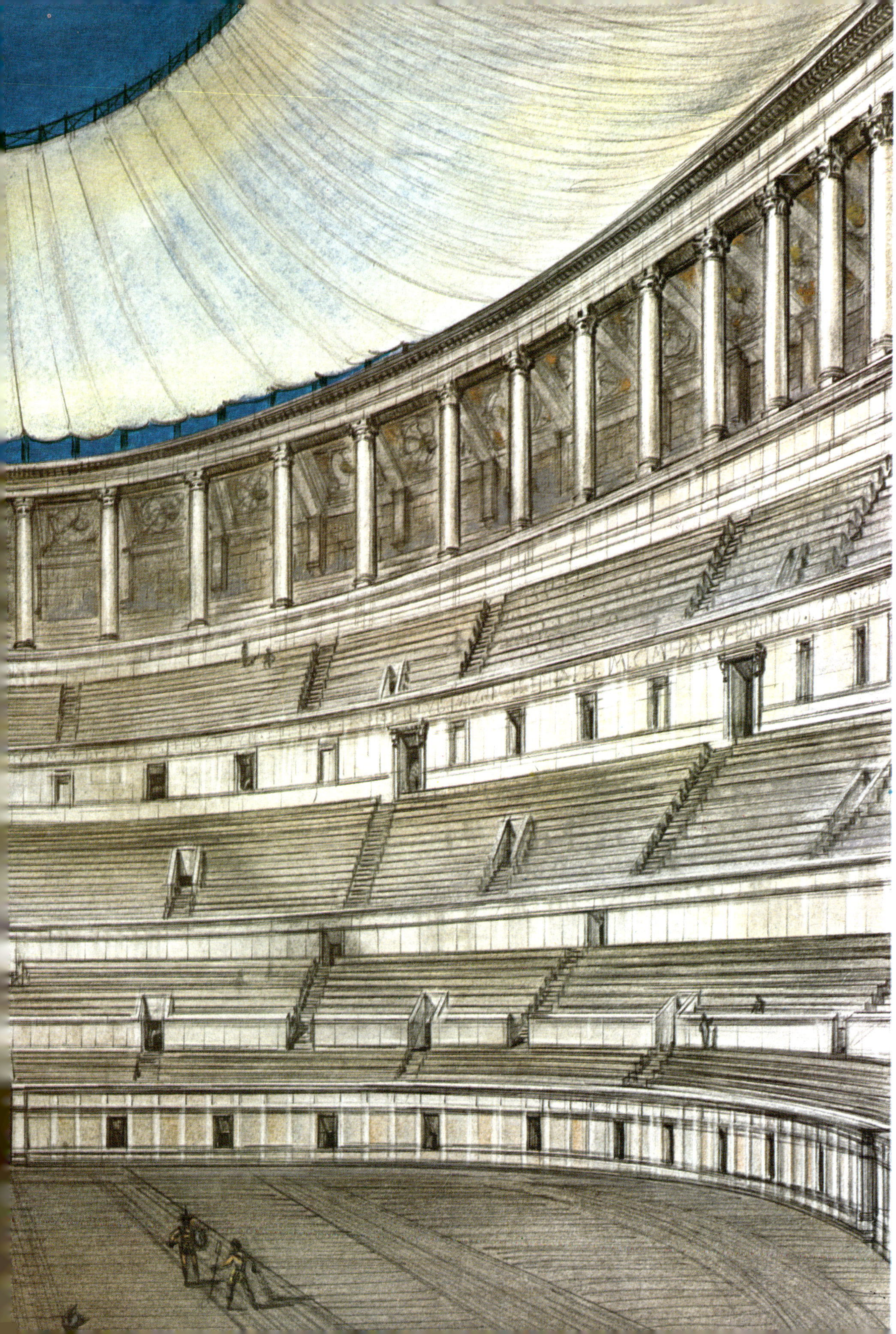

The whole apparatus centred on the great ring like a sort of skylight (1), to which the ropes holding up the canopy were attached. In the first phase, the ring was raised from the arena as far as the level of the cornice (2-6): this operation was carried out with ropes which went from the ring to the pulleys at the top of the poles (3) and from the pulleys to the outside (see detail at the top), being attached to 160 large blocks of stone surrounding the amphitheatre below (4). On each of these blocks there was a winch (see detail at the bottom, 5) with pulleys for rolling up the ropes. The 160 winches were turned in perfect unison to the beating of time, and this was what raised the ring. When the ring was raised, the ends of the ropes were pulled up and tied to the poles (7).

In the second phase, a second rope was lowered from each of the poles and attached to the ring at a level lower than the first rope (8-9): this lower series of ropes, tightened by other pulleys and winches (8-10) on the terrace of the top gallery (summa cavea), formed a sort of spider's web which held up the canvasses of the velarium. These converging sections were unrolled from above, tied to each other, until they reached the central ring (see the upper part of the design, 12).

Only sailors who were extremely expert in handling rigging were capable of carrying out such a vast and complex operation, which also required careful training of the greatest precision not only in measuring and placing the various parts of the velarium and the machinery, but also in the distribution of the men and their tasks and in their timing. The detachment of 100 sailors from the fleet of Misenum, who lived in barracks near the amphitheatre, must have been employed exclusively in the maintenance of the velarium: at least a thousand others were needed to raise and lower it, and they arrived on ships twice a year either at the mouth of the Tiber or at Rome's river port.

If all these requirements are taken into account, along with the enormous surface of the velarium, the huge weight of the ropes and sails and the static and dynamic problems created by resistance and tension, it must be concluded that raising the canopy was a much more difficult undertaking than erecting an obelisk.

The action of the wind was also calculated: it passed both through the central ring and under the

The velarium of the Colosseum (p. 77). Right: drawing of the apparatus for raising the canopy, indicating the successive phases and details of how the tightening of the ropes functioned. (Study and reconstructions by the Architect A. C. Carpiceci).

◀ **Pages 72-73: reconstruction of the interior of the Colosseum. Note the poles for the velarium at the top. (Compare with illustration, p. 68).**

Pages 74-75: interior of the amphitheatre, with the velarium raised. (Study and reconstruction by the Architect A. C. Carpiceci).

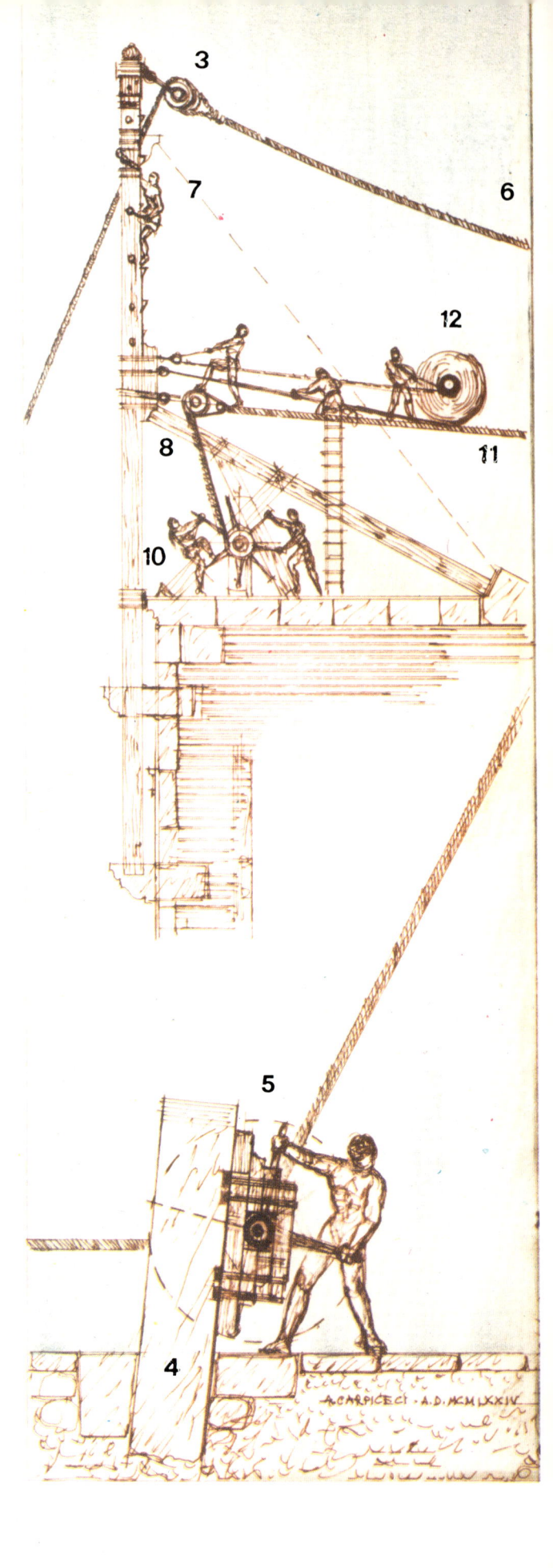

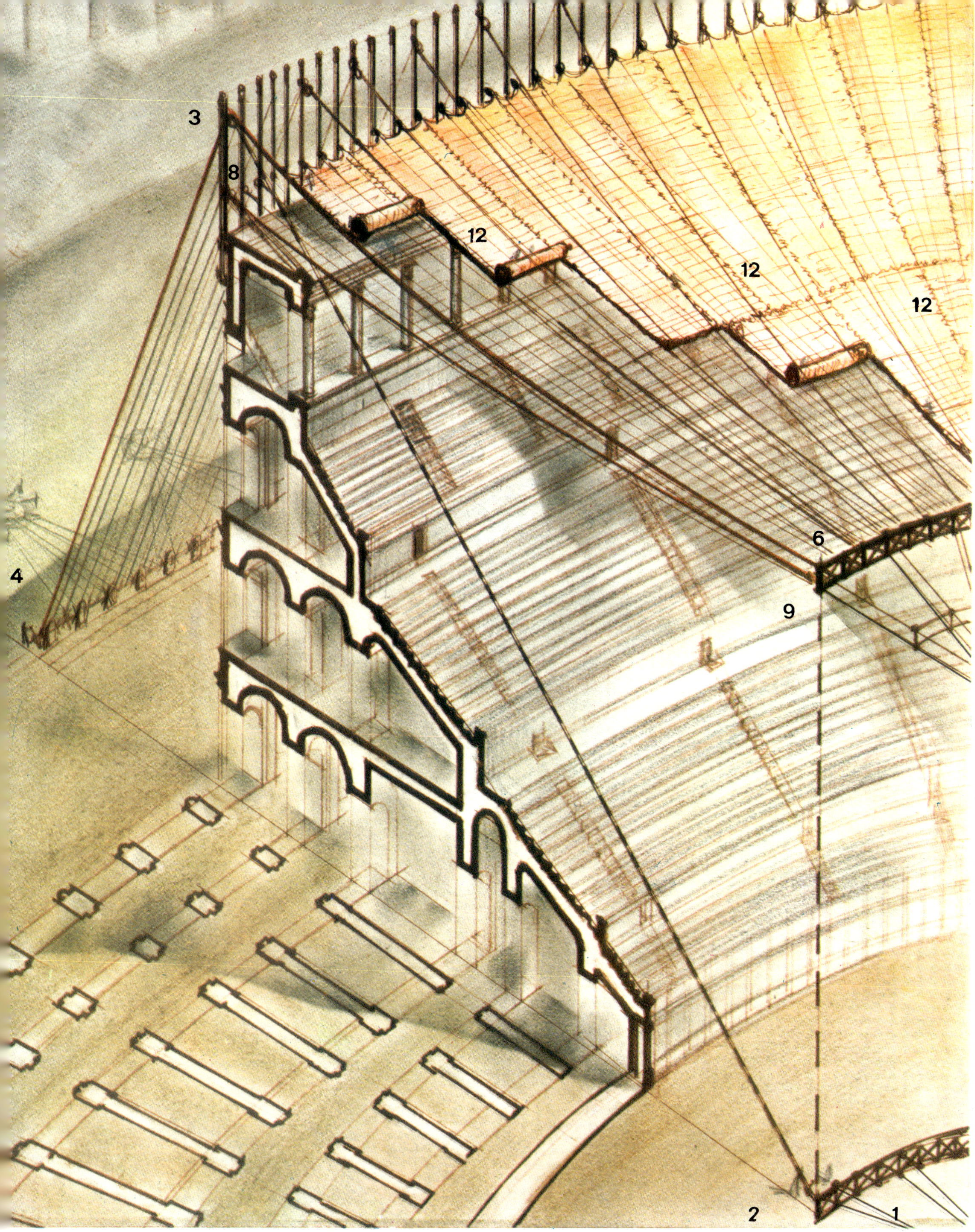
3
8
12
12
12
4
6
9
2
1

Underground structure of the Colosseum: detail of the reconstruction.

external rim of the canopy. Nevertheless, as the historical sources tell us, when the wind was added to the roar of the wild beasts and the uproar of the spectators, an indescribable din was created.

It is strange, to say the least, that there is no indication of the creator of this grandiose work, which inspired admiration and wonder from the time of its construction, and that none of the classical writers, including Martial, who was historian of the Flavian Emperors, made any mention of the subject.

To have a full idea of the difficulties which had to be overcome to build the amphitheatre, mention should be made of the material used, which was for the most part travertine and consequently had to be transported from the quarries near Tivoli to the construction yards.

About 3½ million cubic feet of stone were used in the construction, and these must have required the use of at least 50,000 wagons during the four years which are believed to have been necessary for the erection of the pillars and the framework itself of the Colosseum.

It is therefore believed that about 200 wagons and 400 oxen must have been used every day to move the material.

During these four years, every day, on the Via Tiburtina there were a third of these wagons travelling fully loaded from the quarries to Rome, a third of them travelling empty from Rome to the quarries, and the other third stationary, or rather waiting to be loaded with the blocks of travertine.

It should be remembered that each of the blocks which form the base of the Colosseum's pillars measures 70 cubic feet and weighs five tons.

Amphitheatre scene: gladiators struggle against wild beasts (relief now at Villa Albani).

The spectacles in the amphitheatre were of two sorts: combats between gladiators and " venationes ", or hunts of wild beasts. The animal hunts took place in the morning and the fights between gladiators in the afternoon. Domitian, Trajan and Hadrian had a great love for these sorts of spectacles and often took part themselves. Hadrian stepped into the arena and succeeded in killing a lion with his own hands. To celebrate his triumph over the Dacians, Trajan staged combats which involved 11,000 wild beasts and 10,000 gladiators. Antoninus Pius had tigers, elephants, crocodiles and hippopotami brought into the Colosseum, and introduced a hundred lions in a single day.

But the most magnificent spectacles were staged under the emperor Commodus. He himself may have been the son of a gladiator, rather than of his official father, Marcus Aurelius, and thus have inherited the gladiator's nature. He attended the gladiatorial school, or " Ludus ", and boasted that he had defeated 1000 gladiators.

The occasions on which the games were held could be classified as ordinary and extraordinary. The ordinary occasions were the anniversary of the Emperor's birthday and days on which historical events were celebrated; the extraordinary occasions were to celebrate a triumph or a victory; even funerals were a reason for the staging of spectacles.

Appropriate notices or edicts advised the people of the order of the games, the reason for which they were being held and the day on which they were to begin.

We might conclude with Martial: " Memphis can cease extolling the barbaric Pyramids, because now the wonder of the world is the Flavian Amphitheatre ."

Castrensian Amphitheatre, near S. Croce in Gerusalemme: reconstruction (2nd century A.D.). It was a modest amphitheatre, in which spectacles were probably staged for soldiers from the nearby barracks. In the 3rd century it was incorporated in the Aurelian Walls and the arches of the part outside the walls were filled in.

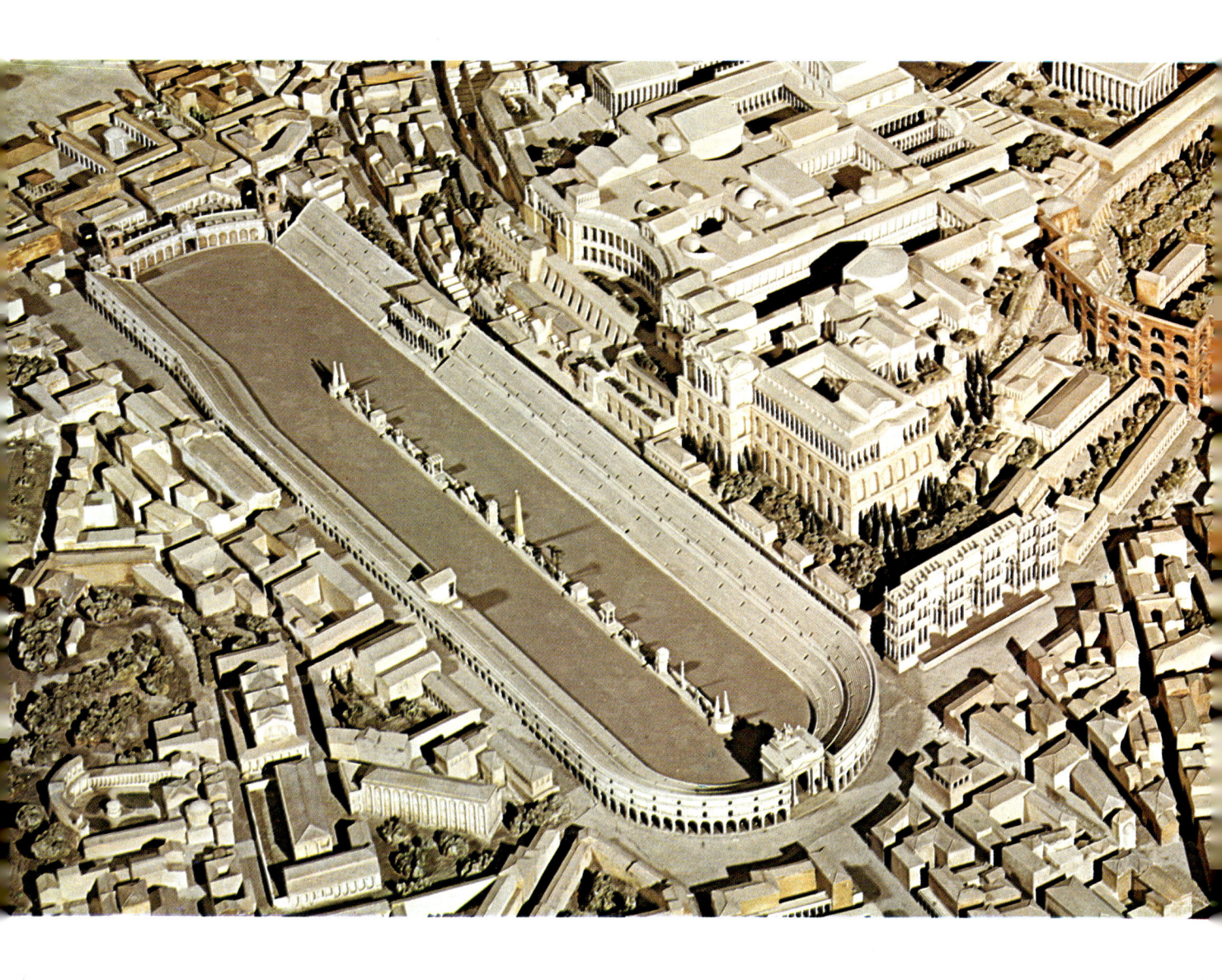

THE CIRCUSES

The extent of the passionate love for horse-racing in ancient Rome can be well understood from the abundant testimonies, rich in details, which have come down to us and which enable us to relive in spirit these contests staged two thousand years ago.

Rome had four circuses, to mention the most important. The Circus Maximus was of extremely ancient origin and had in any case acquired its basic facilities by 329 B.C. with the construction of the permanent " carceres " or starting stalls, followed by the gradual architectural development of the Circus in general. Then in 221 B.C. the Circus Flaminius was constructed, in the first century A.D. that of Caligula and Nero, and finally the Circus of Maxentius on the Via Appia. The circuses had a long, narrow racecourse, divided in the centre by the so-called " Spina ", which was decorated with statues, obelisks, etc. The seating areas occupied the long sides and one of the ends in a semi-circular plan, whereas the other end was occupied by the " carceres ", at the sides of which were two towers.

The Circus Maximus was the most famous and the largest of them: its seating capacity has been calculated at around 250,000 people; the spina in the middle was decorated with two great obelisks, which are now in Piazza del Popolo and the square of St. John-in-Lateran.

Measuring 650 yards long by 220 yards wide, the Circus Maximus seen from outside had three superimposed arcades covered with marble; the

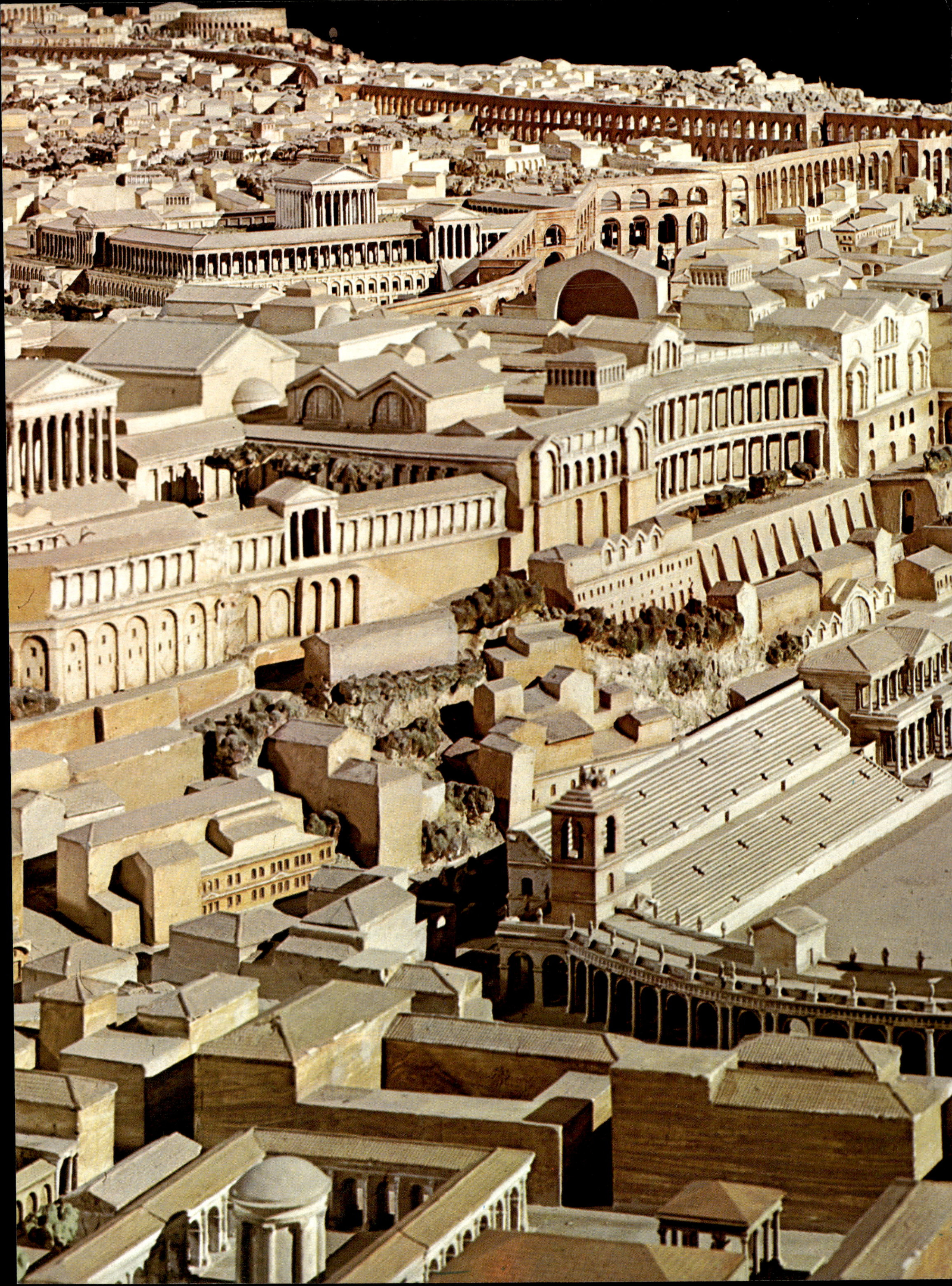

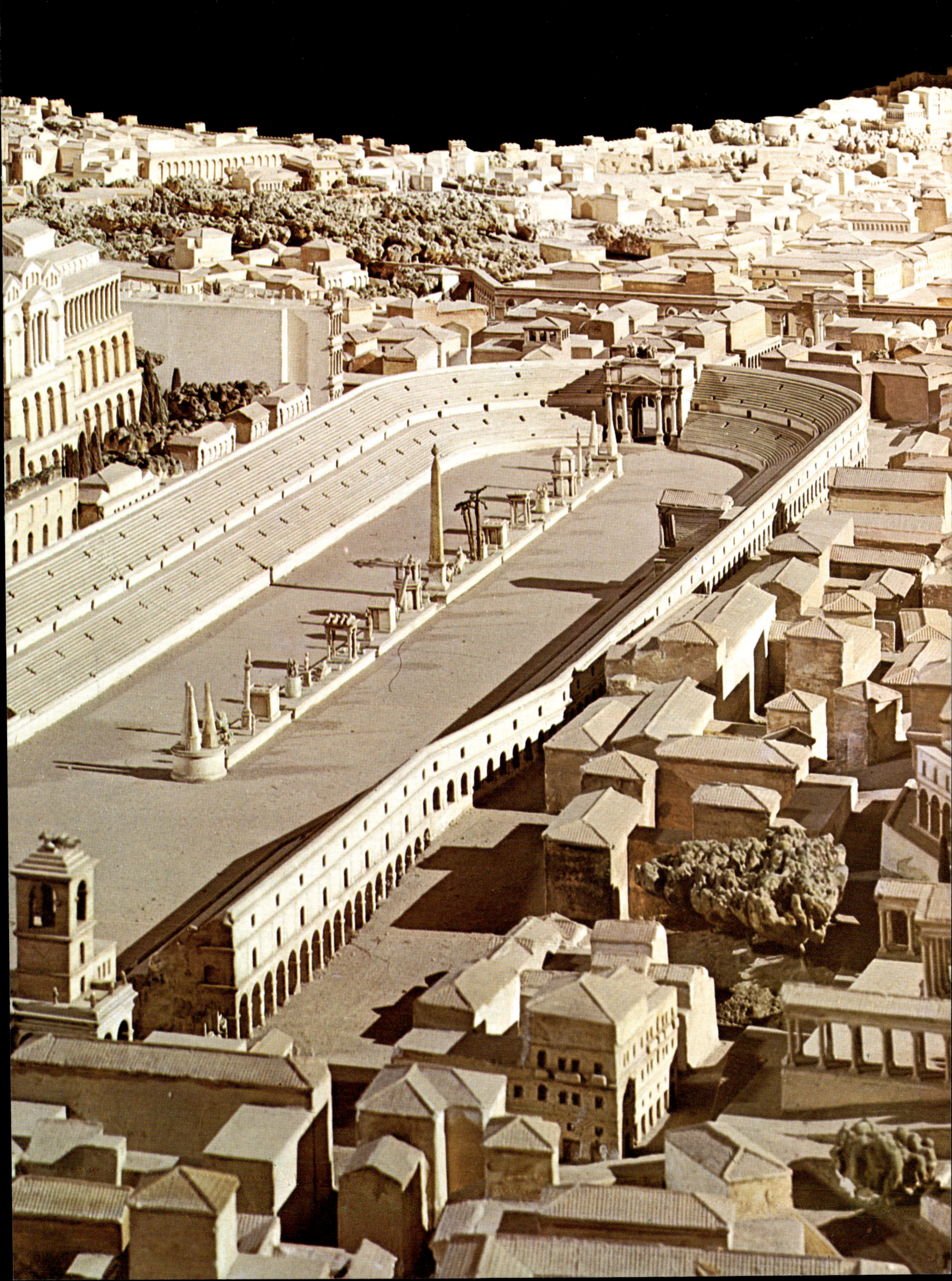

Circus Maximus: reconstruction.

The Circus Maximus today.

arches at ground level were occupied by taverns, wine-sellers and other merchants. The interior, with its great size, filled the visitor with wonder. The first section of the seating area was made of stone while the upper two sections were of wood. On the curved side was the entranceway, consisting of a triumphal arch with vaults, erected in 81 A.D. by order of the emperor Domitian in honour of Titus.

On the opposite end were the starting stalls, from which the signal for the beginning of the race was given.

The spina was some 233 yards long and each chariot had to complete seven laps of the course, which meant a race of about 1600 yards or nearly a mile. At the end of the spina were the " metae ", or turning posts, and seven bronze eggs and seven dolphins. Along the spina were the shrines of the god Consus and the goddess Pollentia and other statues of divinities which favoured the sports, as well as the two obelisks already mentioned.

During the rules of Caesar and Augustus, spectacles including elephants were also staged, and for this purpose Caesar, besides enlarging the Circus itself, had the course surrounded by a ditch filled with water to protect the spectators.

From the abundant testimonies which have come down to us, it is estimated that the Circus Maximus was used on about 240 days a year, so many were the festivities or excuses invented by the Romans for holding horse-races in all possible shapes and forms. In fact, the charioteers not only had to be able riders but also had to perform prodigious feats of balancing, jumping from one horse to the other in races for " bigae ", or two-horse chariots, picking up a cloth from the ground at full gallop, or standing up on the horses' backs. Every possible means was exploited in order to make the races more difficult and thus more interesting.

We know that under Augustus 12 races a day were held; under Caligula there were as many as 34 a day and under the Flavians no less than 100. All the Romans and visitors to Rome came to the Circus. This was the meeting-place of Roman society, including the Emperor. The races in the Circus were so popular that they became one of the most common motifs in Roman figurative art: mosaics, bas-reliefs, statues, even sarcophagi reproduced both general views and particular moments and personalities from the spectacle.

The most famous stables were those of the Reds, the Whites, the Greens and the Blues. The charioteers, because of their great ability, were vied for at enormous prices. Although of humble social origin, they achiev-

The horse races in the Circus Maximus in two reliefs from the Museum of Foligno (top) and the Vatican Museum (above).

The Circus of Maxentius on the Via Appia (beginning of 4th century A.D.).

ed glory and riches. In a short space of time, no more than six or seven years, they could earn astonishing figures. One charioteer by the name of Diocles, after having won 3000 races for two-horse chariots and 1450 for " quadrigae ", or four-horse chariots, retired towards 150 A.D. with a fortune of 35 million sesterces, equal to several million pounds or dollars today. It should be remembered, however, that the fame of the charioteers was due not only to their physical capacities, but also to the risks they ran: in fact most of them died at a very early age.

Particular care was taken of the horses and their training; all of them had their pedigrees, and their popularity was so immense that it reached the farthest

Circus of Caligula and Nero in the Ager Vaticanus (middle of 1st century A.D.): reconstruction.

corners of the Empire: a mosaic has been discovered in Africa with this fervent declaration of love for the noblest of animals:

" Whether you win or lose, we love you, Polidoxus. "

The best-preserved of the Roman circuses is the Circus of Maxentius on the Via Appia. Built by Maxentius in 309 A.D., together with a temple-tomb in honour of Romulus, his son who died while still a boy, the Circus was dedicated to the deceased youth. Measuring 550 yards in length and 85 yards in width with a 305 yard long spina, it was decorated with statues and the obelisk which today rises in the middle of the Fountain of the Rivers in Piazza Navona.

Piazza Navona, once the Stadium of Domitian.

Stadium of Domitian

The stadium derives from a Greek structure resembling a circus, but lacking the starting stalls and spina. It was used mainly for gymnastic events and games. Caesar and Augustus built a wooden stadium in the Campus Martius which was restored by Nero and then reconstructed by Domitian in brickwork and stone in 86 A.D. as headquarters for the Capitoline games. The arena measured 775 yards long (half as long again as an Olympic-sized stadium) and 55 yards wide. The tiers, with room for 20,000 persons, rested on two orders of arcading which made up the external façade, a section of which near the curving part towards the Tiber has been discovered. In the 3rd century, after a fire broke out in the Colosseum, the stadium was temporarily used as an amphitheatre. Destroyed during the Middle Ages, it served as the foundation for the buildings put up around Piazza Navona (from *agone,* " contest ") which perfectly retained its shape and size.

Next to the stadium at the curved part where the entrance was, Domitian also built an Odeon, or small theatre, in which musical shows and poetry readings were staged. It could hold up to 8000 spectators.

Both the Stadium and the Odeon had highly noteworthy architectural decoration, to which Apollodorus of Damascus is supposed to have contributed. They were pointed out as being among the seven wonders of Rome up until the 5th century.

Stadium of Domitian in the Campus Martius (end of 1st century A.D.), today Piazza Navona: reconstruction.

THEATRES

Historical evidence of the activity in the theatres is scanty, although we know that, from as early as the 3rd century B.C., Greek theatrical works were presented in Rome. The construction of the first theatre dates from 179 B.C., a work ordered by the censor M. Emilius Lepidus (Theatrum ad Apollinis). Another was built in 154 B.C. by the censor M. Valerius Messalla and Cassius Longinus, but it was destroyed by order of Scipio Nasica.

It should be noted that these theatres were wooden, temporary structures: the Senate had prohibited not only the construction of permanent theatres, but even the attendance at them by seated audiences, because this was not in keeping with the dignity of the Romans.

Reconstruction model of the Campus Martius with the Theatre of Marcellus (top), the Theatre of Balbus and Theatre of Pompey with the Portico of a Hundred Columns (in the centre), and the Odeon of Domitian (at bottom).

Theatre of Marcellus today.

91

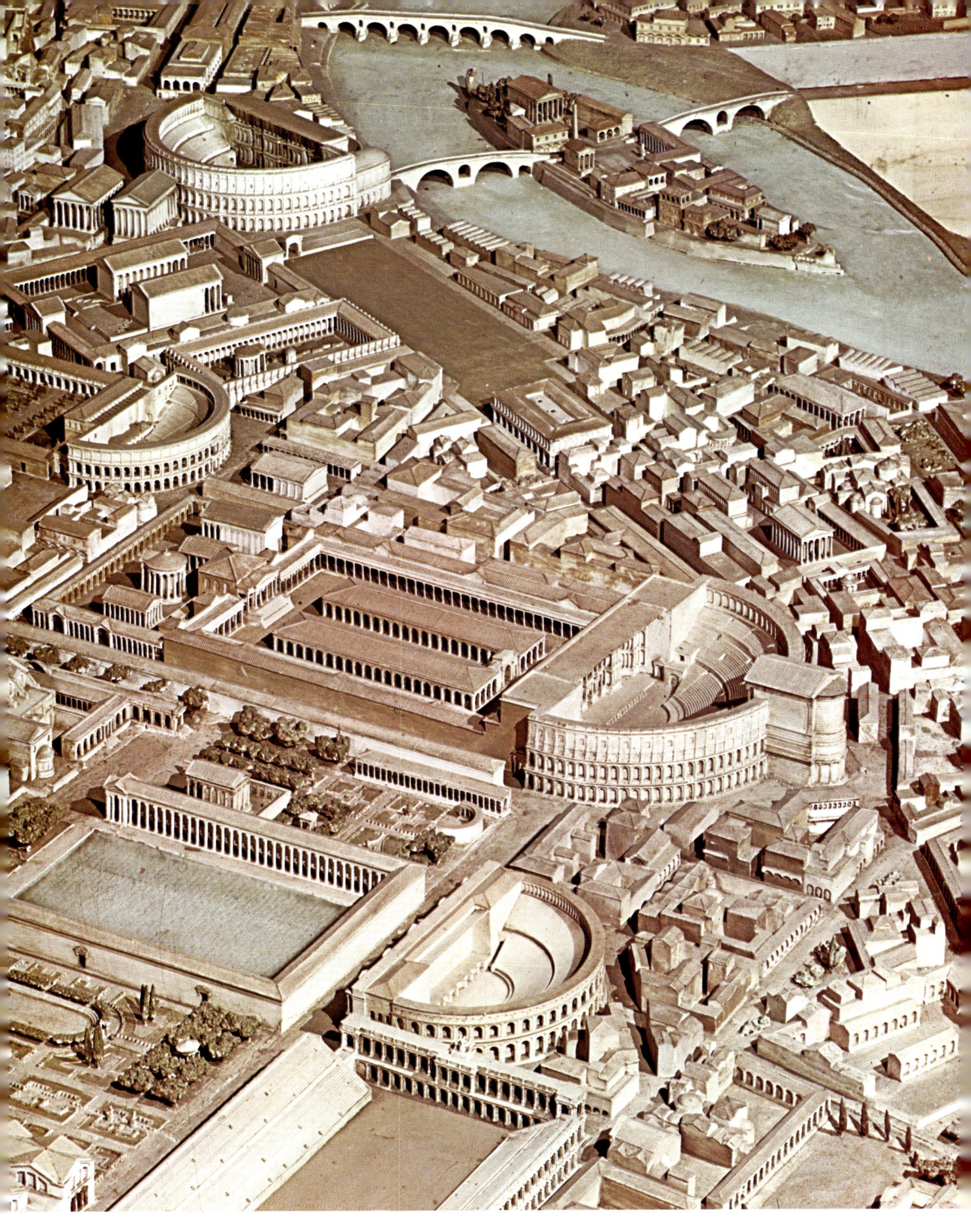

However, we have evidence that there was richly painted scenery (Claudius Pulchrus, 93 B.C., and M. Scaurus, 58 B.C.). The first permanent theatre was built for Pompey the Great in 55 B.C., and in order to circumvent the law which prohibited its construction he had a temple built and dedicated to Venus Victrix above the seating area.

It had a diameter of 520 feet and was capable of accommodating 35,00 people, 28,000 of whom had seats. It was situated between what is now Via di Grotta Pinta and Campo de' Fiori and in front of it was the imposing Portico of a Hundred Columns. Later, in 13 B.C., the Theatre of Balbus was built, with a capacity of some 12,000 people, including 8000 seated. Finally, in 11 A.D., the Theatre of Marcellus was constructed; it was begun by Caesar and completed by Augustus. It had a capacity of 20,000, 15,000 of whom were seated.

The Roman theatres were free-standing constructions, in contrast with the Greek theatres which were cut into the slope of a hill. The external, semicircular part of the theatre consisted of a series of superimposed orders of arches, an interesting and practical solution both from the engineering and aesthetic points of view. The stage was in contact with the seating area and the wall at the end of it was of the same height as the seating area.

Unfortunately it must be said that the dramatic art for which these theatres were built was not at the same level as their grandiose dimensions and capacity, and indeed was in a state of decadence both in Rome itself and in all the provinces of the Empire.

The last tragedies were presented not later than the time of Augustus. Nor were the special prizes, introduced to encourage their production and presentation, sufficient to avoid this decline.

What was then the entertainment of the masses, the Circus, the equivalent of today's football, had emerged victorious.

The last word can be left to Pliny the Younger, who deplored the Romans' desertion of the theatre, their abandonment of tragedy for the Circus sports: " Not only does the mob give importance to the colours of some wretched jockey's silks, even more wretched than they are, but so do those who believe they are distinguished, who define themselves as serious.

" When I think about this futile, stupid and monotonous entertainment (horse-racing), I derive a certain joy from the fact that I get no joy at all from the races! "

Theatre of Marcellus (end of 1st century B.C.): reconstruction model.

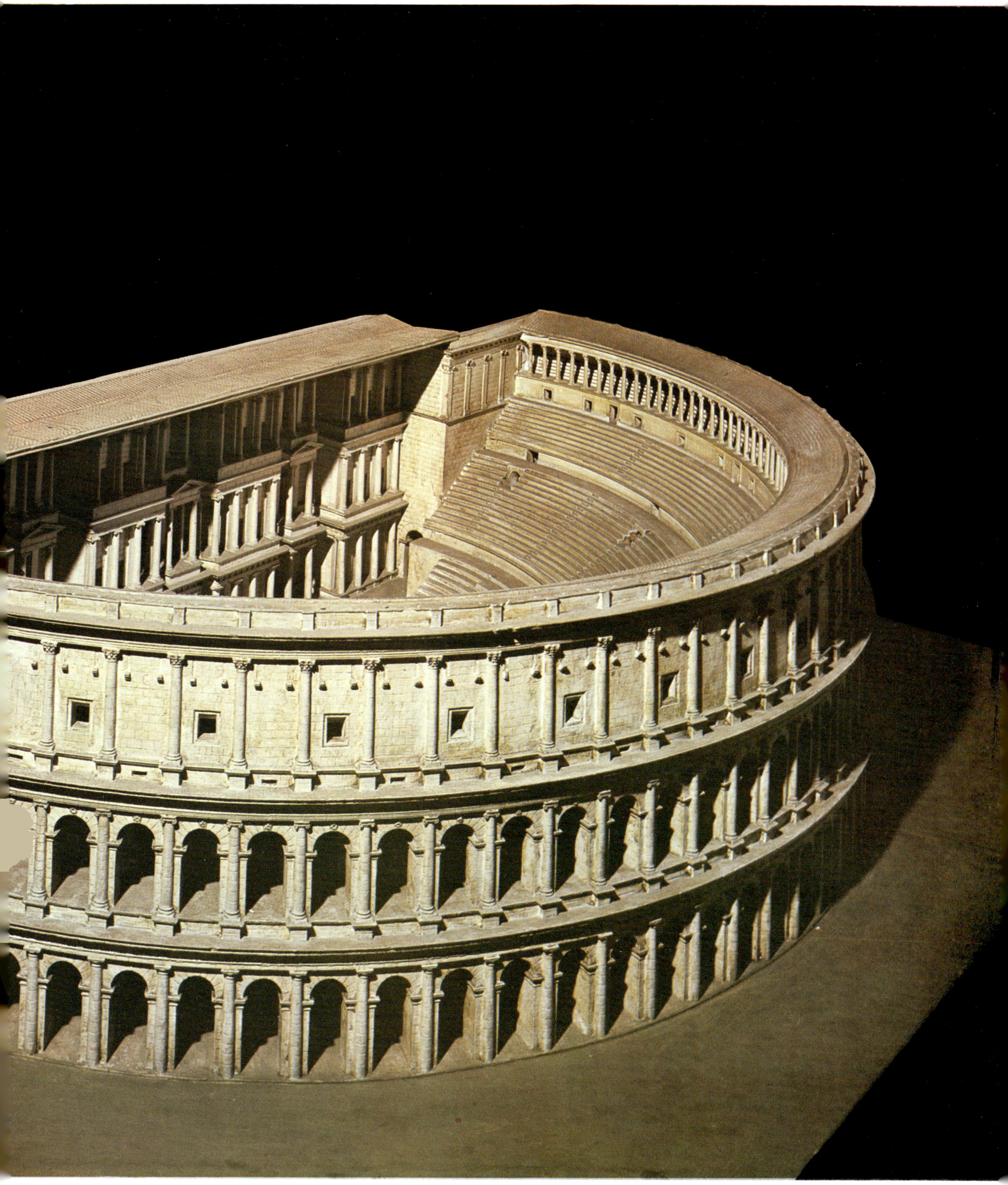

THE TIBER, ITS ISLAND AND BRIDGES

The construction and maintenance of the bridges over the Tiber was indispensable for the life and commercial traffic of the city of Rome and for the people who lived to the north and south of the city.

Tradition has it that the construction of bridges ("pontes" in Latin) was entrusted to a college of "pontifices" which later became the most important of the religious orders; thus Varro and Dionysius maintain that "pontifex" (in Rome a high priest, now used for the Pope) originally meant builder of bridges. These builders, of whom there were five, were from the earliest beginnings of the city the guardians of a store of proven technical wisdom and experience in the construction of bridges.

The first historical bridge was the Pons Sublicius. Its name derives from its "sublicae", or wooden piles, and it was located downriver from the Tiberine Island; the memory of Horatius Cocles is linked to this bridge. Later, to give it greater stability, the wooden piles were replaced by stone piers, the wooden arches being retained since the use of iron was prohibited for religious reasons.

Aerial view of the Tiberine Island today, with the Ponte Cestio, the Ponte Fabricio and the one remaining arch of the Ponte Emilio (Broken Bridge).

The first stone bridge was the Pons Aemilius, built in 179 B.C. It was followed by the Pons Fabricius, 62 B.C., and the Pons Cestius, 60 B.C., which formed a permanent link to the Tiberine Island. These last two bridges have come down to our times, the first almost intact while the second was arbitrarily rebuilt last century with blocks of travertine.

The Tiberine Island was the site of the Temple of Aesculapius, erected towards 291 B.C., and it became a place reserved for the treatment of the sick; the temple can be considered to have been the

Reconstruction of the Tiberine Island and left bank of the Tiber (at right, the Theatre of Marcellus and temples of the Forum Olitorium; at left, the Ponte Emilio).

first primitive hospital in Rome.

Later come the Pons Aurelius, the bridges of Agrippa and Nero, the Pons Aelius (Ponte Elio, or bridge of Hadrian), still in use though its external arches have been modified, and the Ponte Milvio. Throughout the Middle Ages, until the construction of the Ponte Sisto (1473), the Roman bridges at the Tiberine Island and the Ponte Elio and Ponte Milvio were the only links between the two banks of the Tiber.

The banks of the Tiber were kept free of buildings to leave room for the wharves where boats tied up.

In the Campus Martius was the naval dockyard (Tccstrinum), while the commercial port was situated in the vicinity of the Boarian Forum and consisted of a basin, quadrangular in form and closed in by seawalls. An important unloading point for materials, marble and foodstuffs was the Emporium. On the site of the Emporium, terracotta vases (testae) discarded by cargo ships accumulated over the centuries into an artificial mountain, known as Testaccio.

Such intense traffic, the activity of the docks and shipping, must have given particular animation to the Tiber. In addition, there were at least four Naumachiae built along the riverbanks. These were huge, amphitheatre-like structures which contained enormous pools for sham naval battles and other spectacles on water.

Many idlers passed the time watching the arrival and departure of the boats. A description has come down to us of the arrival of the Imperial ship, loaded with booty from Macedonia, on which Paulus Aemilius reached Rome among the crowds which flocked the riverbanks.

THE BATHS

An old Roman proverb defining an ignorant man said: "He doesn't know how to read or to swim." One of the highest expressions of the might and civilisation of Rome lay in the construction of its numerous baths. From their earliest times, the Romans had private baths in their houses and villas, and at Rome there was a public swimming-pool, which gave its name to the 12th District and where the Romans learnt to swim.

Leaving aside the minor baths, such as the Decian and Suran baths and those of Maecenas, the Imperial baths in chronological order were those of Marcus Visanius Agrippa, the son-in-law of Augustus, Nero, Titus, Domitian and Trajan. The Baths of Trajan marked a new point in the development of the design of thermal baths because of their disposition with a central complex of buildings and an enclosure around the perimeter, and the addition of gardens and "exedrae" (open meeting-places), so that they became the model for all the others which followed. These included the baths of Commodus (185 A.D.) of Caracalla (217 A.D.), of Diocletian — the largest (303 A.D.) — and finally those of Constantine (326 A.D.).

The Baths of Antoninus or of Caracalla (beginning of the 3rd century A.D.), today and in a reconstruction model.

An estimate based on various sources indicates that in ancient Rome at the beginning of the 4th century A.D. there were 11 public baths, 926 private baths and about 2000 fountains. The huge quantity of water necessary to supply them was furnished by no less than 14 aqueducts.

To form an idea of what the baths were like, the baths of which such imposing ruins remains today, we must examine the Baths of Caracalla which give us an almost complete overall view at least of the central body of this important structure.

Marcus Aurelius Bassianus was born at Lyons on 6 April 186 A.D. of Julia, the beautiful second wife of Septimius Severus. He was given the ironic nickname of Caracalla by the people because he was of Gallic origin and wore the Gallic dress, a long cape with a hood called the " caracalla ".

He followed his father, the emperor Septimius Severus, in his compaign against the Parthians, and during this war, at the age of 11, he was proclaimed Augustus, that is successor to his father. For the campaign against Judaea, the Senate decreed that he should be given the triumphant title of " Pius Felix ". On the death of his father, which occurred at Eboracum (York) in 211, Caracalla and his brother Geta became emperors. Whereas Geta was an inept, underhanded deceiver, Caracalla in his youth had a docile, friendly character and was gifted with considerable intelligence. Unfortunately he contracted a chronic form of illness which completely changed his character, so much so that he had his brother killed.

Baths of Caracalla: mosaic with grape-gathering putto.

Baths of Caracalla: mosaic with geometrical motifs and acanthus spirals.

The first act of his reign was to confer Roman citizenship on all the free men in the Empire. In 217, during a campaign against the Parthians, he was killed (plot of Macrinus). Later he was buried in the Mausoleum of Hadrian. His great achievement was the construction of the enormous baths, and this more than his military undertakings earned him his place in history.

The baths were begun by Caracalla in 212 A.D. and were inaugurated in 216 A.D. The inauguration was performed by the emperor himself, who was the first to bathe in them. However, it should be added that they were only completed under Heliogobalus (218-222 A.D.) and Alexander Severus (222-235). Capable of accommodating 1600 bathers, the baths were considered a perfect architectural work. In fact, they were admired for many centuries. They fell into abandon from the 6th century on, and were reduced to ruins as a result of the raids of the Saracens in the 11th century. In the Middle Ages they became veritable quarries of marble and building materials. Among the many objects discovered during excavations here were the Hercules and the Farnese Bull, the Callipige Venus and the Flora, now in the National Museum of Naples; the Chiaromonti Venus and the Belvedere Bust, now in the Vatican; the Dionysus in the British Museum; the baths on the fountains in Piazza Farnese and many other works scattered throughout the museums of Rome, including the Capitoline and National Museums.

The baths were quadrilateral in form, with an outside measurement of 368 yards in width and 369

Statue called the "Belvedere Torso" (now in the Vatican Museum), found at the Baths of Caracalla in the 16th century.

yards in length, thus occupying a total area of some 135,000 square yards. The central body of the structure, inside the enclosure, measured 241 by 233 yards. The baths were built on a line running from north-west to south-east. On the front there were four entrances, two on each side. The exterior was surrounded by majestic covered porticoes. Between the entrance and the central building there was a spacious garden surrounding the building itself on three sides.

The interior was subdivided in a rational and functional way. The central building had four entrances on the front and two on the sides. Between the two central entrances in the façade, there was a vast rectangular hall used for cold baths (Frigidarium), a hall which was not covered but surrounded by a gallery above for spectators; this gallery was supported by eight granite columns 48 feet high and 5ft 3in in diameter (see the column of Piazza S. Trinita in Florence). The gallery was adorned by statues standing in 18 niches and by bas-reliefs. On each side of the Frigidarium, there were two dressing-rooms and two rooms for oiling the body before physical exercise, followed by two conversation rooms. Then came an enormous hall which occupied the centre of the baths complex, surmounted by a cruciform vault supported by huge pillars, among which there were four pools for warm-water baths; among the decorations of this area were eight black granite columns with splendid capitals, besides mosaics and stuccoes. In the centre was the shower, or "lavatio".

This area was called the "Tepidarium"; from the Tepidarium the bathers passed through an intermediate area to reach the "Calidarium". This was a circular area 55 yards in diameter with an internal gallery supported by twelve granite columns, a large cupola resting on eight pillars and pipes running along the walls for the radiant heating. This hall contained seven pools for hot baths and the central part served as a "sudatorium", or sweating-room. The remaining part of the baths, along the sides of the central complex, consisted of a series of rooms used for physical exercises, rooms with warm baths, sweating-rooms, libraries, two gymnasiums or peristyles, rectangular halls with columns all the way around forming a portico, with mosaics on the floor and the walls covered with marble. A row of old-gold columns divided these halls from the exedrae, on the long sides, which were covered with marble and mosaics. The floor consisted of a splendid polychrome mosaic depicting athletes, discus-throwers and acrobats. This was discovered in 1824 and transported almost complete to the Lateran, to be transferred later to the Vatican where it is today.

On three sides of the external enclosure, between the enclosure and the central complex, after the Calidarium came a magnificent stadium with trees and gardens, halls for walking in, academies, small exedrae for philosophers, and libraries; this was where the Aqua Marcia aqueduct, carrying the water used in the baths, entered.

Excavations have established that there were some 3 miles of tunnels intersecting beneath the baths, and have also permitted us to understand the internal hydraulic system and the ventilation and drainage systems. In addition to these various systems, there was also a sanctuary to Mithras in the underground zone.

We have described the Baths of Caracalla because we believe that, in the end analysis, the language of the ruins themselves is more eloquent than any commentary. In fact even from this brief description it can be seen that the baths were planned and built to comply with that concept, still sought after in our own civilisation today, which is so admirably expressed in the Latin motto: *Mens sana in corpore sano* (A healthy mind in a healthy body).

Baths of Diocletian (298-306 A.D.): reconstruction model. They were the largest in Rome, with a surface of some 1,210,000 square feet, and were capable of accommodating more than 2000 bathers. It should be noted that the present-day Piazza della Repubblica follows the lines of the exedra which faced the Calidarium (at right in the reconstruction).

101

IMPERIAL MAUSOLEUMS

The Mausoleum of Augustus today.

Mausoleum of Augustus

Caesar Augustus had his Mausoleum erected in 28 B.C. It had a circular plan, based on the design of the Etruscan tombs, and measured about 295 feet in diameter and 137 feet in height. Centred on a cylindrical pillar on which stood a gilt bronze statue of the Emperor, it then had a series of concentric, ring-shaped galleries, covered with vaults. Around the central pillar, the burial crypt was created. Access to the Mausoleum was by a corridor which ran through the ring-shaped galleries until it reached three niches, one opposite the entrance and two at the sides, in which were the urns of the Imperial family. Here were buried Marcellus, Caius and Lucius, nephews of the Emperor; Agrippa; Octavia, his sister; Drusus; Germanicus; Livia, his wife; and then Tiberius, Caligula, Claudius and Nerva. Much later,

Julia Domna, the wife of Septimius Severus, was also buried here.

At the entrance to the Mausoleum there were two pink granite obelisks, one of which is now in Piazza dell'Esquilino and the other on the Quirinal fountain. Beside the entrance, fixed to two pillars, were the tablets of bronze on which the political testament of Augustus was inscribed. The bronze plates themselves have been lost, but the complete text of the testament of Augustus has come down to us in the copy inscribed on the walls of the Temple of Rome and Augustus at Ankara *(Ancyra)*. That is why this illustrious historical document is often called the *Monumentum Ancyranum;* it is transcribed in bronze letters on the modern base of the Ara Pacis in Via Ripetta.

The Mausoleum of Augustus in the reconstruction model.

Castel Sant'Angelo, originally the Mausoleum of Hadrian; at bottom, the modern Vittorio Emanuele bridge.

Mausoleum of Hadrian

Towards 130 A.D. the emperor Hadrian constructed for himself and his successors the mausoleum known today as Castel Sant'Angelo. The mausoleum was completed a year after Hadrian's death, which occurred in 138 A.D. It consists of a square base 295 feet long on each side and 50 feet high, above which stands the drum or cylindrical body, divided inside by radiating walls covered with vaults. The upper part was covered with earth and cypress trees, and at the top there must have been a bronze four-horse chariot, or the statue of the Emperor.

The exterior of the mausoleum was covered with travertine and the interior with marbles and stucco decorations; the cylindrical base and the summit of the monument were adorned with marble and bronze statues. The enclosure around it was decorated with a series of bronze peacocks, two of which can still be seen in the Vatican. The funerary chamber was reached by a spiral stairway. In the mausoleum were buried Hadrian, his wife Sabina, Antoninus Pius and his wife Faustina, Lucius Verus, Marcus Aurelius, his son Commodus, and Septimius Severus and his son Caracalla. The monument was transformed into a defensive fortress from as early as the time of Aurelian and it became the keystone of the defensive system on the right bank of the Tiber.

The Mausoleum of Hadrian (132-139 A.D.): reconstruction model with the Aelian Bridge as it still was at the end of last century; at the bottom, the Bridge of Nero, no longer in existence.

CITY WALLS AND GATES

The Aurelian Walls mark the beginning of the end for Rome. The increasing menace of the barbarian invasions convinced the emperor Aurelian to build an adequate circle of walls for the city. The building of this imposing structure was begun towards 272 A.D. Its perimeter is about 12 miles long, and the walls included the entire city with the exception of a few areas on the extreme outskirts.

In the building of the walls, many pre-existent works along their course were included or exploited as defensive structures, such as the walls of the gardens of the Acilii (Muro Torto, or Crooked Wall), the Castrum Praetorium, the Aqua Marcia and Aqua Claudia aqueducts, the Castrensian Amphitheatre and the pyramid of Gaius Cestius.

The original height of the walls was about 25 feet, but in later works of reconstruction it reached as much as some 32 feet. The material used was brick, though in later reconstructions a variety of materials was used. Incorporated into the walls were the towers, equipped for defensive weapons; these rose every 100 feet, and it is estimated that there were a total of 383; the walls also had about 2000 windows and numerous posterns.

The Aurelian Walls could also be called the Walls of Honorius because of the important works of reconstruction and transformations carried out by this emperor (395-423 A.D.).

There were fourteen main gates: the *Porta Flaminia* (Porta del Popolo), over the road of the same name, consisted of a barrel-vault flanked by two towers which were destroyed at the time of Sixtus IV (1471-1484). The present-day appearance of the inside of the gate dates back to the time of Pius IV (1562-1565) and the outside to 1655, when Bernini carried out works for the visit of Queen Christina of Sweden, whereby its original appearance was somewhat modified. Morever, it was enlarged, with the addition of the two minor archways, in 1879.

The present-day *Porta Pinciana* was constructed by Honorius from a postern dating from the time of Aurelian. The Via Salaria Vecchia passed through it, linking up further on with the Via Salaria.

The *Porta Salaria* had a barrel-vault with two towers of the type built by Honorius, but it was demolished after 1870, following the damages caused by the entry into Rome of the Italian Army. During its demolition, two burial-places dating from the time of Augustus came to light: one belonging to a twelve-year-old poet, Q. Sulpicius Maximus, and the other to a woman called Cornelia.

The *Porta Tiburtina* was constructed in one of the archways supporting the Aqua Marcia, Aqua Tepula and Aqua Julia aqueducts at the time of Augustus (5 A.D.). The arch had two round rather than square towers, and on the attic were the bronze statues of two emperors (Arcadius and Honorius).

The *Porta Prenestina*, or Porta Maggiore, was a monumental display of the Claudian and Aniene Nuovo aqueducts, later incorporated in the walls. It stood at the beginning of the Via Labicana and the Via Prenestina: the most recent work of restoration in 1957 has brought to light the remains of the doors and some paving-stones of the two roads.

The Porta Appia (today the Gate of San Sebastiano) in the Aurelian Walls.

◀ **The Aurelian Walls (271-275 A.D.), in the section between the Ardeatina postern and the Porta Appia.**

The *Porta Asinaria* was also originally a small Aurelian gate, but was transformed under Honorius by the construction of its towers and second door: it was damaged by a fire at the time of Robert the Guiscard in 1084 (hence called the Porta Perusta, or Burned Gate).

The *Porta Metrovia,* situated on the side of the Coelian Hill, was a gate of modest dimensions at the time of Aurelian, but was rebuilt later and equipped with an internal tower on the vault of the gate itself.

The *Porta Latina* originally had a much larger passageway, but Honorius reduced the size of the arch for security reasons and added the attic.

The *Porta Appia,* or Porta di San Sebastiano, was originally built by Aurelian with two archways, but Honorius and Arcadius transformed it into its present state by reducing it to a single archway and by heightening and reinforcing the towers, besides exploiting the so-called Arch of Drusus (one of the supports of the Antoninian aqueduct) as a second door. Not far away there was a postern: the Ardeatina.

The *Porta Ostiense* originally had two archways, but these were reduced to one by Honorius and Arcadius; beside it there was a postern. The towers were built at the time of Maxentius. The second door, which also belongs to the time of Maxentius, retains the two original archways of the gate. According to the historian Ammianus Marcellinus, the obelisk brought to Rome by Constantius II in 357 and erected on the spina of the Circus Maximus was transported through the Porta Ostiense.

The Aurelian Walls also included a section on the other side of the Tiber, in which there were three gates:

The *Porta Aurelia* was situated near what is today the Porta San Pancrazio: it consisted of a single archway with two square towers, and was equipped with a second door. It was demolished in 1644 under Pope Urban VIII during the reconstruction of the walls between the Tiber and the Janiculum.

The *Porta Settimiana* was reconstructed by Pope Alexander VI in 1498.

The *Porta Portuense* was about 500 yards south of the present-day Porta Portese; it had two archways and two round towers. It was demolished by Pope Urban VIII in 1643 and replaced by the Porta Portese for reasons of economy and security.

The Porta Ostiense (today Gate of San Paolo) in the Aurelian Walls, with the Pyramid of Gaius Cestius, a funeral monument dating from 12 B.C., later incorporated in the walls.

AQUEDUCTS, FOUNTAINS AND NYMPHAEA

The aqueducts are of great interest in the study of Rome's town-planning. An examination of the course taken by them and the network which they created allows us to identify and establish the various zones of the city. The writer Frontinus (1st century A.D.) tells us that at the time of Nerva the aqueducts carrying water to the city were the Appia, Aniene Vecchio, Marcia, Tepula, Julia, Vergine, Alsietina, Claudia and Aniene Nuovo. Later came the Trajana and the Alexandrina.

For the first four hundred years after the foundation of the city, the Romans used only water from springs, wells and the Tiber. There were many springs, the most famous of which was the Camenae Spring, near the Porta Capena.

As the city developed and the population increased, it became necessary to provide a greater quantity of water. It was the censor Appius Claudius Caecus, the same man who built the so-called "queen of roads", the Via Appia, who in 312 B.C. constructed the first aqueduct, bringing to Rome the water named Aqua Appia after him. The spring from which the Aqua Appia came was about 10 miles east of Rome; the greater part of the aqueduct was built underground and only as it neared Rome itself was it placed on arches. The aqueduct which came next after the Appian was the *ANIENE VECCHIO* (Old Aniene), built in 272-269 B.C. It was about 25 miles long and brought to Rome the water of the Aniene, a tributary of the Tiber, from a point near the present-day town of Vincovaro. It too was an underground structure, consisting of a canal cut into the rock.

The aqueduct carrying the *AQUA MARCIA* was built in 144-140 B.C. by the praetor Quintus Marcius Rex and was about 36 miles long. The springs serving it were near Subiaco and its water ran for about 30 miles in an underground canal, then for the last 6 miles on arches. It served the Campidoglio, Coelian, Quirinal and Aventine areas of the city.

The *AQUA TEPULA* aqueduct, built in 125 B.C., was about 11 miles long and brought its water from the Albani Hills; it was underground for the first 6 miles, while for the last 5 miles it ran on the same arches as the Aqua Marcia.

The *AQUA JULIA* aqueduct, built in 33 B.C. by M. Vipsanius Agrippa, was about 12 miles long and its spring was near that of the Aqua Tepula on the Albani Hills. Half its course was underground and the other half ran over the same arches as the Marcia and Tepula aqueducts.

The *AQUA VERGINE* was the second aqueduct to be built by Agrippa in 19 B.C. It was about 13 miles long, entered Rome via the Pincio and terminated at the Baths of Agrippa in the Campus Martius.

Augustus in 2 B.C. constructed the aqueduct for the *AQUA ALSIETINA* (piped from Lake Alsietino, now called Lake Martignano). Its water was used only for irrigation. In 52 A.D. the emperor Claudius built a new aqueduct from Subiaco to pipe to Rome the *AQUA CLAUDIA*, which reached the Coelian Hill and then continued on to the Palatine for the Imperial Palaces. Claudius also completed the acqueduct called the *ANIENE NUOVO* (New Aniene): it entered Rome by the Porta Maggiore on the same structure as the Aqua Claudia.

Trajan in 109 A.D. constructed an aqueduct north-west of Rome, which drew its water from several springs in the vicinity of Lake Bracciano. It was about 27 miles long and terminated in Rome on the Janiculum.

Finally, in 226 A.D., Alexander Severus constructed the aqueduct which brought to Rome the water from the springs east of the city, near the Via Prenestina. This water served for his baths in the Campus Martius.

The Roman aqueducts represent the greatest triumph of hydraulic engineering not only in Roman times but in all history.

Moreover, after the building of the aqueducts, which were capable of meeting all practical necessities, the city could also be embellished with fountains and nymphaea. Of the fountains of ancient Rome, some were erected as decorations for buildings, but others consisted of self-contained monuments, as for example: the *Meta Sudans* from the time of Domitian (82 A.D.), the *Lacus Orphei*, mentioned by

◀ **The Claudian Aqueduct between the Palatine and Coelian hills.**

The Septizonium of Septimius Severus: reconstruction model.

A section of the Aqueduct of Claudius near the Via Latina.

Martial as being on the Esquiline, the *Lacus Ganimedis,* the *Lacus Promethei* and the *Septizodium,* built by Septimius Severus (203 A.D.). Monumental fountains were also constructed as displays of the aqueducts; this was true of the complex called the Trophies of Marius (though it actually belongs to the time of Domitian) on the Esquiline, consisting of a high façade divided into two levels, with a large central niche and two openings at the sides, in which were the trophies, while there was a circular pool at the bottom into which the jets of water fell. The so-called Porta Maggiore is in fact the display of the Claudian Aqueduct.

The fountain was called by the Romans LACUS or NYMPHAEUM. The "lacus" was often a rectangular basin with a practical use. At the time of Agrippa there were more than 500 of them, and he added another 700, adorning them with 400 columns and statues. During the rule of Domitian, statistics tell us that no less than 1350 fountains existed in Rome.

ROADS AND COMMUNICATIONS

The practical sense of the Romans when it came to roads appears clearly if one examines the reasons which led them to travel. Originally the Romans built their roads for exclusively military and political reasons. The legions were responsible for their building and maintenance. From Rome there were 29 roads fanning out to link the city with the provinces, and they continued on into the countries across the border, crossing the Alps. These were called consular roads, and they were in turn linked to each other by the secondary or provincial roads.

The roads usually had a central strip for vehicles and the animals which pulled them and raised footpaths at the sides for pedestrian traffic. These were the roads along which the Roman post ran, permitting the Emperor to deliver his orders to the farthest corners of the Empire in the briefest possible time. The public service which served to transport the persons and things belonging to the State constituted the Imperial post, a foreshadowing of the later idea of organised tourism.

It should be noted that the costs involved in the post were borne by the provinces and that these were particularly heavy: they included the maintenance of the various buildings, " mansiones " (inns), " stationes " and stables, and of the numerous and varied personnel involved, the workers, muleteers, veterinarians, carpenters, stable-hands and drivers. Besides this, the provinces also paid for the feeding and upkeep of the men and animals.

Obviously, anyone who could not make use of these State services had to turn to private enterprise. As a result, alongside the State organisation which had been created for military and political reasons, private organisations soon sprang up prepared to affront the risk of travel and transport, hiring carriages and animals and assuming the responsibility of delivering private post. For land transport, various sorts of vehicles were used. Guides and itineraries for travellers (tourists) have been written in fact since the most ancient times (Deliciae Siciliae, Mirabilia Rhodensia, Mirabilia Urbis Romae, etc.).

Stops were made about every three miles and about 18 miles were covered a day. At every stop, the traveller could slake his thirst or find refreshments in the taverns which grew up alongside the postal offices of the Empire. Towards evening he would reach the station where, if he was not in the service of the State and could thus not make use of the official inn, he sought lodging in the private inns.

We know that the companies of private hotel-keepers formed a union and that there thus existed strong business ties between them, so much so that travellers could have a hotel card issued by the travel agencies, which might be defined as the prototype of our travel vouchers.

The Via Appia Antica.

The Via Appia

The Via Appia was planned and its construction as far as Capua supervised by the censor Appius Claudius, called Caecus (" blind "), in 312 B.C. It is the longest, widest and finest of the Roman roads. In fact, it was called by Statius the " queen of roads ". Its construction was dictated by military needs, as was that of all the Roman consular roads. To build it, difficult obstacles had to be overcome: it had to cross the Pontine Marshes, valleys, large and small streams and mountains. It was paved with polygonal slabs of basalt brought from the hills of Latium; Julius Caesar restored and embellished it, meeting the costs personally; and Augustus, Domitian, Vespasian and Nerva made further restorations and added other embellishments. From Capua it was extended first to Benevento and then as far as Taranto and Brindisi; Trajan opened up another route from Benevento by way of Canosa and Bari (the " Via Appia Traiana "). This project was celebrated in reliefs on the Arch of Benevento, the most beautiful of the Roman triumphal arches. The Via Appia began from the gate called the Porta Capena, which no longer exists today; for about the first 12 miles it was lined on both sides by the tombs of Rome's most important citizens, including the Sepulchre of the Scipiones and the Sepulchre of Geta, the brother of Caracalla who barbarously killed him. We know that the emperor Caracalla had this sepulchre built with seven levels or orders of columns. In the vicinity of the Catacombs of San Callisto were the sepulchres of the Pomponia family and the columbaria (sepulchres with niches) of the Imperial cooks and the sailors from the fleet at Misenum who raised and lowered the Velarium on the Colosseum.

In the area around the Catacombs of San Sebastiano was the Mausoleum of Romulus, son of the emperor Maxentius, and beside it the Circus of Maxentius. It measured about 550 yards in length by 85 yards in width and could accommodate about 18,000 persons. The spina was 305 yards long and was decorated, as was the custom, with statues and with the obelisk which is now on the Fountain of the Rivers by Bernini in Piazza Navona.

The tomb which, because of its imposing appearance and relatively good state of preservation, at least on the outside, has been most identified with this consular road is that of Cecilia Metella, standing at the top of a short rise at the third mile on the Via Appia. It consists of a quadrangular base above which stands the cylindrical body of the monument. It is about 65 feet high and covered all over with blocks of travertine; high up there is a frieze of ox-skull and garland motifs in Pentelic marble and under this is the tablet commemorating Cecilia Metella, daughter of Quintus Metellus Creticus, the general who conquered the island of Crete and was awarded a great triumph for this feat. Cecilia married the son of the triumvir Licinius Crassus, the richest man in Rome.

At right, the Tomb of Cecilia Metella (1st century B.C.) on the Appia Antica.

OSTIA - THE PORT OF ROME

The literary origins of Ostia are linked to the legendary landing made here by Aeneas. Other literary sources suggest that its foundation dates back to the time of Ancus Marcius, fourth king of Rome. However, from archeological discoveries it has been possible to show that the foundation of Ostia coincides with the issuing of the first Roman coin, that is towards 335 B.C.

The historical evidence of Ostia during the Republican period is scanty, but we know that in 278 B.C. the Carthaginian fleet tied up at Ostia, sent to help the Romans in the war against Pyrrhus. During the Punic Wars, Ostia played an extremely important part: in 217 B.C. provisions were shipped from Ostia for the Roman army which was then in Spain; in 212 B.C. grain brought from Sardinia was unloaded there; in 211 B.C., P. Cornelius Scipio sailed from Ostia with thirty quinqueremes.

From these few scattered facts, it can be seen that the beginnings of Ostia coincided with the beginning of the maritime and commercial policy of Rome.

At first a fortified citadel, it later became a larger city surrounded by new walls with a perimeter wide enough to accommodate the port's development during the Imperial period.

It is believed that its conversion from "citadel" to city occurred towards 267 B.C. when its quaestor was appointed, or rather when the political and administrative structures of Ostia were created.

In the light of recent excavations, the character of the city towards the end of the Republican period appears to have been that of a commercial centre. Lining the main streets there were rows of shops and the modest houses of the people, alongside more luxurious dwellings of the type with an atrium and peristyle; in many cases, along the streets there were porticoes with columns of travertine or pillars of tufa. Beneath the streets were sewage systems. Outside the walls were the cemeteries, or necropoles.

At Ostia as in Rome, urban development was linked to the evolution in the use of building materials, and it was thus in the Imperial period that the city underwent a complete transformation from the point of view of town-planning.

From as early as the Republican period, Ostia had been considered the "emporium", or commercial centre, of Rome, and the strengthening and expansion of its facilities, which had to meet the needs of Rome itself, was therefore indispensable. In fact, intense building activity commenced under Augustus, and the theatre and the Forum of the Corporations, which was to become the commercial centre of the city, came into being. Later Tiberius constructed the Forum and the Temple of Rome and Augustus.

◀ **Ostia - Reconstruction of blocks of apartment buildings and shops (Insulae).**

Ostia - Ruins of the so-called House of Diana.

The increased shipping traffic made the delta of the Tiber insufficient, and in 42 A.D. Claudius began the construction of a real port, which was to be completed by Nero in 54 A.D.

Unfortunately this port was not entirely satisfactory, because it was too exposed to the sea and its maintenance was extremely costly. For this reason Trajan between 100 and 106 A.D. built a new and much more functional port inland; it was hexagonal in form and was linked to the Tiber by means of a new waterway (the "Fiumicino", or little river) and to the city of Ostia itself by a double roadway.

Under Trajan construction activity become more intense; large storehouses were built to contain foodstuffs: grain, oil and wine. New buildings such as the Basilica and the Senate were added to the city. Under Hadrian and Antoninus Pius (117-161 A.D.), Ostia was completely reconstructed and transformed by new town-planning projects which took into account, as well as the public buildings, the citizens' residential areas; the city's dwellings were changed from the type with atrium with its horizontal development in favour of vertical development, that is houses with several storeys, receiving their illumination from outside by means of windows in the façades, on the street and on open internal courtyards, until finally came the construction of garden houses, the dream of every modern town-planner.

Other projects realised in this period were the reconstruction and enlargement of the Capitolium, as well as the reconstruction of the area around the Baths of Neptune, and the building of the Police and Firemen's Barracks.

Septimius Severus and Caracalla (203-217) supervised the renovation and enlargement of the Theatre, which had been begun by Commodus (180 A.D.). At the same time, the Forum of the Corporations was renovated. This was the most interesting complex in the city: in the middle stood the Temple of Ceres, the goddess who protected cereals and foodstuffs; all around it was a portico, along which were the offices of the commercial organisations of Ostia and of other cities in the Empire, such as Carthage, Sabratha, Narbona and Alexandria, the names of which can be read in the mosaics of the pavements.

Ostia - Top, the main decuman road and the theatre; bottom, the Synagogue.

Ostia - Capitolium.

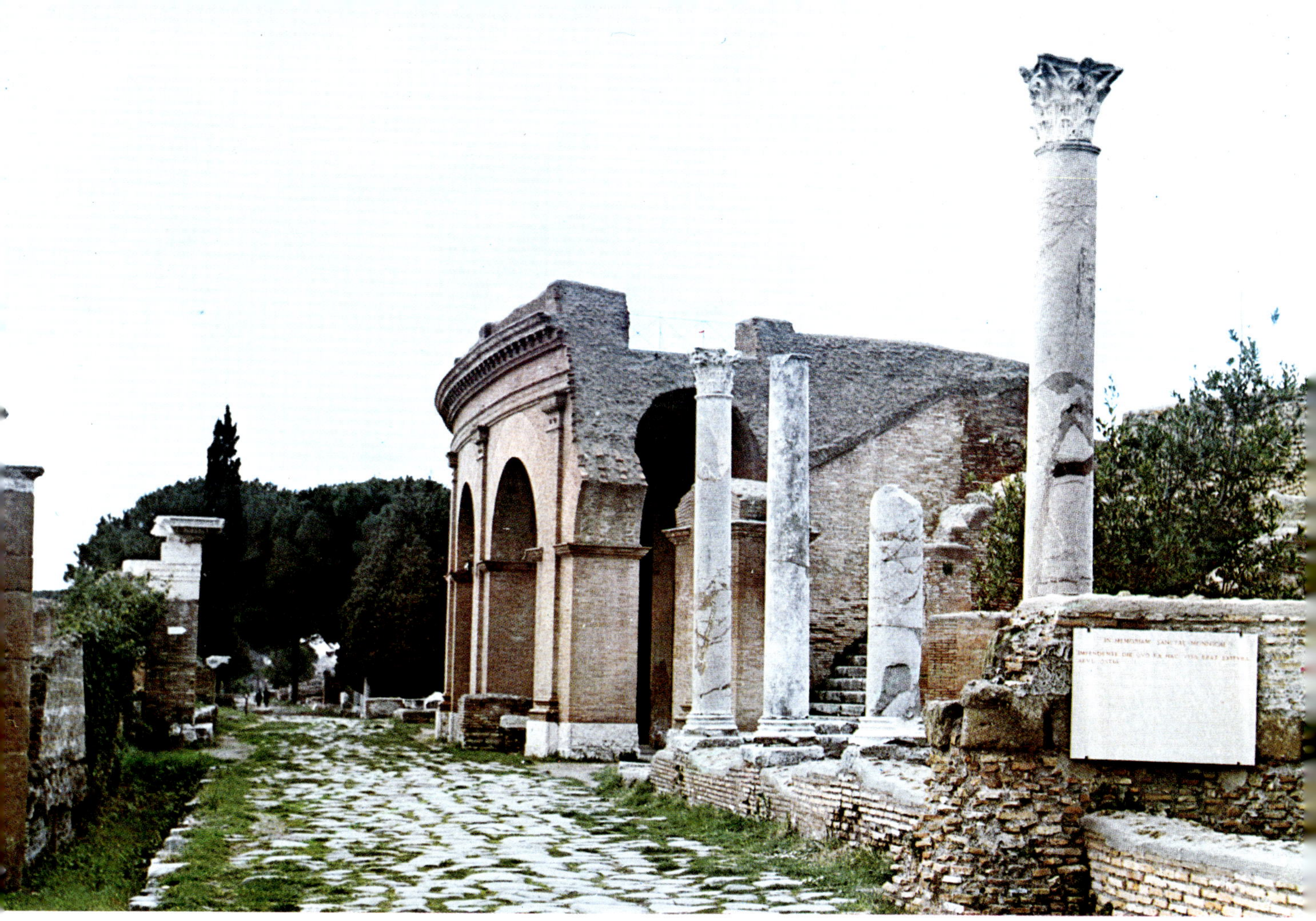

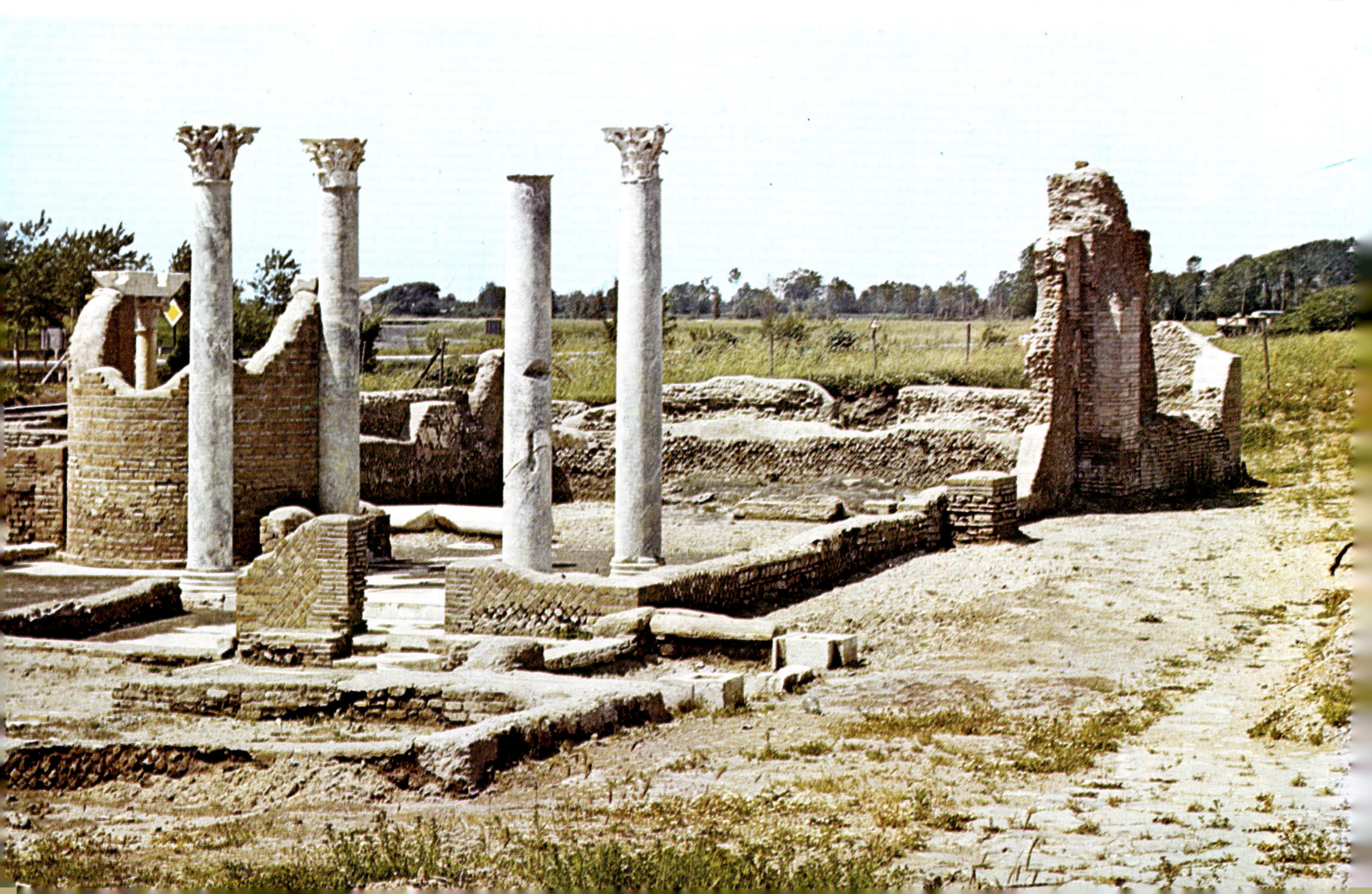

Ostia - the theatre with the Forum of the Corporations and remains of the Temple of Ceres.

This was in fact a veritable chamber of commerce, a meeting place for merchants of skins, ivory and cloth, for artisans, sailors and bankers.

It can be said that throughout the 3rd century A.D. there was a continuous process of building and development at Ostia, and the additions to the city included the baths, storehouses, " fullonicae " (laundries), temples, Mithraic sanctuaries, blocks of houses for rent, the headquarters of professional organisations, and so on. The population of Ostia reached 50,000 inhabitants, and it was a heterogeneous and cosmopolitan population.

Magistrates and State officials were responsible for organising and controlling the distribution of foodstuffs and checking their quantity and quality, as well as making payments and maintaining contacts with private and State commercial representatives. At the same time, they had to maintain discipline among the various associations of workers: those employed in the dockyards repairing ships; those who unloaded the ships; the masons responsible for the upkeep of the wharfs in the port and those used by the ferries; and even the divers who recovered the cargo of sunken vessels. Moreover, they had to maintain contacts with the owners of ships and other means of transport.

The decline of Ostia can be said to have begun under Constantine, who devoted his interest exclusively to the port and abandoned the city to its own devices.

Towards the end of the 4th century A.D., St. Augustine, having reached Ostia with his mother, St. Monica, who was to die in an inn while waiting to sail for Africa, had occasion to note with bitterness the demise of the city. Later, the poet Rutilius Namatianus (414 A.D.) confirmed the fact that nothing was left of Ostia except the glory of Aeneas.

TIVOLI AND HADRIAN'S VILLA

A few miles south-east of Rome, at the foot of the hills which lead up to Tivoli, the old city which was one of the favourite resorts of the aristocracy and poets of ancient Rome, is Hadrian's Villa. It should be noted that "Hadrian's Villa" is actually an enormous complex of buildings which the emperor Hadrian erected between 118 and 138 A.D.

This vast complex, the remains of which have been excavated, must have covered an area of at last 750 acres, of which only 150 acres remain today as State property.

The name "Villa" is thus inadequate as an indication of the size and magnificence of this Versailles of ancient Rome.

In order to understand the spirit in which it was conceived, one has to have some knowledge of its creator.

Aelius Hadrianus was born at Italica, a pleasant little town on the coast of the Mediterranean in Spain. He was a cousin of the emperor Trajan on his father's side. A great lover of Greece, he took up the studies, the way of life, the language and indeed the entire culture of the Athenians; in fact he came to be called the " little Greek ". He was musician, doctor, mathematician, philosopher, poet, painter, sculptor, and above all architect. He had a virtually encyclopedic mind and a prodigious memory: he remembered everything, from places and facts to the names of soldiers. His physical capacity was also exceptional, and in fact he crossed the provinces of the Empire on foot. His army consisted of blacksmiths, carpenters, builders, architects and all sorts of other workers, whom he organised into divisions like the legions.

Wherever he went, he left his beneficial imprint, restoring, beautifying and fortifying the cities he visited.

He was never the same, because he had a many-sided personality. Among his many gifts, he was also a born military leader. But often he preserved a state of peace with minor kings by means of secret favours, even though he was harshly criticised for this policy by the Senate.

He maintained the army in a state of perfect efficiency, but always boasted that he had achieved much more by not using the army than anyone else had achieved by wars. He died at the age of 62; prostrated by excruciating pains throughout his body, many times he asked his most faithful servants to put him to death, and his friends had to watch him day and night to prevent him from committing suicide.

Hadrian's Villa near Tivoli (126-135 A.D.): reconstruction model by I. Gismondi and R. Vighi.

This is as much as we know about Hadrian from the writings of Aurelius Victor, who lived about two hundred years after him. But the personality of this emperor remains today as disconcerting as it was for his contemporaries and biographers. Perhaps the idea which most dominated him was that of uniting the heterogeneous people of the Empire's various provinces, of providing for their needs and thus creating internal political unity in order to realise lasting and universal peace.

Hadrian's Villa: the hemicycle of the Pool of Canopus with the statues of Mars and the Amazon by Phidias.

The historian Durvy has written: "Should the glory of rulers ever be measured by the happiness which they have given their people, then Hadrian will have to be considered the greatest of the Roman emperors."

Hadrian's Villa

Building was Hadrian's real passion: he travelled throughout the then known world and built theatres, aqueducts, walls and roads. He reconstructed Jerusalem and restored the city of Athens. The temple which he built at Cyzicus was so splendid that it was considered one of the seven wonders of the ancient world. But one of his finest creations was the villa which he built at Tivoli.

The Villa is unique and is entirely the work of Hadrian. It strongly reflects the mind and spirit of its builder. In fact it is a stupendous book of souvenirs of the travels of Hadrian, a book of recollections of places, of cities and of monuments, such as the Vale of Tempe in Thessaly; the Stoa Poecile, the Prytaneum and the Academy in Athens; and the Serapeum at Canopus on the Nile delta near Alexandria in Egypt. At Tivoli, Hadrian brought to life his recollections and impressions, for he called the various buildings of his Villa by the names of the monuments which had most impressed him.

However, it must be pointed out that the originality of the architecture and the clearly Roman construction methods make it almost impossible to identify

Hadrian's Villa: the great Pool of Canopus with copies made under Hadrian of the caryatids from the Erechtheum of Athens.

most of the monuments in the Villa with the celebrated buildings which inspired them and whose names they bear. Except for the Canopus, all the names should be considered as no more than suggestions useful for a visit.

As well as these buildings, Hadrian built two theatres, complexes of thermal baths, pavilions, peristyles, nymphaea, fountains, cryptoportici, lodgings for the praetorians (bodyguards) and servants and large storerooms. All these structures were distributed rationally, taking advantage of the nature of the terrain, and groups of buildings were alternated with vast open zones left as gardens.

The decorations were sumptuous and highly refined; the marbles, paintings, mosaics and statues were the highest expressions of art, as the infinite number of works which have been discovered here goes to prove. Here, in these incomparably beautiful surroundings, in the company of his friends and of all those who loved poetry, sculpture, philosophy and music, Hadrian passed the last years of his life. His farewell to the world is finely expressed in the verses which he himself wrote:

> My little soul, charming wanderer,
> guest and companion of my body,
> you are leaving now
> for the pale, cold regions,
> and the games with me and my friends
> are over....

The Villa remained in use until the end of the Empire, but fell into ruins during the Middle Ages. Columns, marbles, architraves, floors and even the bricks were carried off. Its works of art, searched for since the end of the 15th century, have been scattered throughout the museums of Europe. The most important masterpieces are in the collections of the Capitoline Museum and Vatican, the Museo delle Terme and Borghese Gallery in Rome, the Louvre in Paris, and in Naples, London, Berlin, Dresden, Stockholm and Leningrad.

For some decades now, the Italian government has been sponsoring the systematic excavation of the site. The restoration of the most important buildings has also been begun and water has been piped back into the pools and fountains, under the supervision of Roberto Vighi. Even though the "Villa" has been only partially excavated up to now, it still offers, through its incomparable beauty, an intuition of the man who conceived and created it.

THE WORKING WORLD IN ANCIENT ROME

After a description, however brief, of the most imposing buildings of ancient Rome, one is naturally led to ask, an understandable question when contemplating the ruins of the past: who were their builders?

At this point, people often think of slaves and their indiscriminate use to realise such projects. But where Rome is concerned it must be remembered that, apart from being celebrated for its laws and its military conquests, it also gave birth to that corporative spirit of which the most splendid example were the " collegia " or professional corporations.

In discussing the organisation of labour among the Romans, emphasis must be given to the importance of these professional organisations, which at times conditioned the city's politics and economy and which played a leading part in the development of the city itself.

Tradition attributes the foundation of the corporations to Numa, the second king of Rome. Originally there were nine: Masons, Dyers, Shoemakers, Goldsmiths, Potters, Tanners, Blacksmiths, Fluteplayers, and a ninth category which included all the other trades.

While the hypotheses which suggest that the corporations had a religious purpose should not be ignored, it can nevertheless be affirmed that from their very beginnings the basic reason for their existence was economic and professional.

The lower classes, the plebeians, from among whom the corporations were mainly drawn, did not come within the constitution and thus formed a

◄ **Hadrian's Villa: small temple of Venus with the statue of Venus of Cnidus by Praxiteles (restored in 1959 by the Friends of Hadrian's Villa).**

Construction works, in a detail from the Column of Trajan.

confused majority with no religious or political rights: this state of religious and social isolation led them, as a necessary gesture of self-defence, to bring the corporative principle into being.

Reliable information about these professional organisations begins to become available in the final Republican period, when they are described as free societies, but potentially organised and having a complex hierarchy. They thus had great political importance because of the large number of votes which they could control.

Each corporation had its headquarters, which was called the "Schola" and where all those who belonged to the body met. The officials who directed the organisation were renewed every five years. Each corporation had its own treasury, which it administered directly, and had the right to possess houses, land, slaves and so on.

The law established that each professional body should have a representative with full powers to represent the corporation itself before courts of law. Because of the political power which it involved, election to the office of representative, or "patronus", of the professional bodies was much sought after, sometimes even by senators.

It was thus of considerable advantage for a worker to become a member of a professional corporation, both because of the protection which he received from it and because of the means thus put at his disposition. In fact the worker who was a member had the right to a share of both the body's normal profits and its income from other sources (bequests or legacies), in proportion to the position which he occupied in the hierarchy of the corporation.

With the passing of time and the expansion of Rome's political power, the number of corporations multiplied, as we know from the considerable subdivision of labour, resulting in an important evolution among skilled and unskilled workers.

The basis for the recruitment of members of the professional bodies was the apprenticeship system. The apprentice, once he had learned his trade, became a member of a corporation to which he had to pay a special entry fee.

This huge organised mass of workers did not meet with the approval of the State, which towards the end of the Republic began to show its hostility towards the corporative principle. Cicero, who at first had sought election in order to obtain its political support, was the first to demand that the body of workers be suppressed. Claudius, whose name was synonymous with agitation, opposed what Cicero demanded and forced the Senate, by threatening a popular uprising, to re-establish the right to form associations and to grant the right of belonging to the associations to slaves and foreigners. This was the first step in the society of ancient Rome towards and equality of rights between slaves and free men in the highly important sector of the workers.

The great conquests in Spain, Africa and Sicily and its commercial and maritime development had enriched Rome, but unfortunately this new wealth was not enjoyed by the corporations of free workers, and indeed they saw their activities curtailed by the competition from numerous slaves and servants who had come to Rome along with the new wave of prosperity. Employed by their owners, the slaves robbed the organisations of free workers of all possibility of employment.

This led to the creation of a new system which was to reduce the liberty of the professional corporations as well as their opportunities of employment.

There emerged powerful merchant groups which acquired a certain number of slaves; these were taught a trade and then their labour was sold to third parties, or else they were employed directly by their owners. The slave was paid a small wage (peculium) as an incentive to work.

But as for the slaves, it should not be forgotten that their condition, within the civic and social context of ancient Rome, was considerably less unhappy and inhuman than it was among other peoples both in ancient times and in the medieval and modern periods. Proof of this are the severe laws which protected them and determined their treatment; the great ease with which slaves were emancipated and, as freedmen, assumed the name of their former owner, often going on to achieve considerable prosperity and even filling important intellectual and political positions; the collective sepulchres, often sumptuous, which the great families erected for their slaves and freedmen; and the endless proofs of fidelity and devotion to their owners and protectors given by the slaves themselves. It was not unusual for freedmen to pay for the funeral monument of an owner who had been reduced to poverty out of their own pockets.

The first two centuries B.C. represent the most prosperous era of the Roman world, when the opulence of Rome reached its peak. The corporations on the one hand and an army of slaves working for their owners on the other made possible the construction of the vast, imposing buildings whose ruins still provoke our astonished admiration today.

THE CATACOMBS

The catacombs were the original burial-places of the early Christians. The original name was "coemeteria", or sleeping places; only one of these cemeteries, that of San Sebastiano, was known by the name of Catacomb; perhaps because the entrance was at the bottom of a depression, giving rise to the hybrid Graeco-Roman expression and origin of the word "catacomb". The expression was extended to all the Christian cemeteries from the 10th century on. The catacombs are all situated outside the old circle of walls, this was in observation of a Roman law that strictly prohibited the burial or burning of any dead body within the city. They consisted of subterranean tunnels with several levels, cut into the tufa stone. Each main tunnel was crossed by secondary tunnels to form a complex network. The extent of these tunnels in the Catacomb of San Sebastiano, reached a length of seven miles. It has been estimated that the 52 known catacombs in Rome, if laid in a straight line, would have a total length of no less than 360 miles.

It has by now been established, contrary to common belief, that the catacombs were used exclusively as the common burial-places of the early Christians and not as hiding places to escape persecutions. It can be stated, however, that the early Christians often met in the catacombs, under the pretext of holding funeral services, to celebrate their religious rites.

The tunnels formed links between *chambers* (crypta) which sometimes contained the tomb of a martyr or were used for the celebration of liturgies or the anniversaries of the dead. These *crypta* were often decorated with stuccoes or expressive paintings in richly contrasting colours. Among these decorations many of the primitive symbols of this new faith

Basilica of SS. Nereo e Achilleo in the Catacombs of Domitilla.

Catacombs of Domitilla: tunnel with "loculi" and "arcosolium".

may be seen: the fish, the olive tree, bread, the palm, the vine, the symbol of eternity, the dove, the symbol of the soul and the ship.

Along the tunnels were rectangular niches in which bodies were deposited; the niche was then closed with a tombstone of marble or some other material. The niches could contain one, two or more bodies and on the tombstones were carved the names of the dead. This type of burial was given the name "loculus". Besides being found along the corridors these are also found in the chapels and even in the walls of the stairs; "loculi" were also dug in the floors during the later period.

The "arcosolia", on the other hand, were tombs in the more exact sense of the word and were often decorated. They owe their name to the fact that above the tomb there was an arch, built or dug out of the tufa. In this case the slab that covered the tomb was laid flat and could be used as an altar to celebrate the Mass.

The catacombs were lit by oil lamps, candelabra and lamps hung from the ceiling but mainly by occasional openings that allowed a weak light to enter from high up; these were probably the holes used to remove the rubble when the catacombs were dug.

The catacombs ceased to be used as burial-places around the 5th century but they remained places of devotion as is shown by the large amount of graffiti left by pilgrims on the tombs of the martyrs. During the 7th century the bodies of the martyrs were removed to the churches and gradually the underground cemeteries lost their use until even the location of the entrance of most of them was forgotten. The only catacombs that were always known and were places of veneration were San Sebastiano, San Lorenzo, San Pancrazio and San Valentino.

INDEX OF PLACES AND MONUMENTS

(The volume's chapters are indicated by capital letters)

Alta Semita: 27.
Altar of Caesar: 27.
— of Peace (Ara Pacis): 6, 38-39, 103.
Amphitheatre, Castrensian: 8, 80, 106.
— Flavian: see Colosseum.
AQUEDUCTS: 106, 109-111.
ARCHES, TRIUMPHAL: 45-52.
Arch of Augustus: 27.
— of Constantine: 8, 49-51, 67.
— of Drusus: 60.
— of Germanicus: 60.
— of Janus: 50.
— of Piety: 40-41.
— of Scipio: 32.
— of Septimius Severus: 8, 17, 29, 48-49.
— of Tiberius: 29.
— of Titus: 16.
— of Titus at the Circus Maximus: 84.
— of Trajan: 66.
— of Trajan at Benevento: 113.
Asylum: 30.
Aventine: 5, 109.

Barracks of Police, Firemen at Ostia: 116.
Basilica Aemilia: 16-17, 20.
— Argentaria: 56.
— Julia: 6, 16, 17, 24, 56.
— of Maxentius: 8, 28.
— of SS. Nereo e Achilleo: 125.
— Ulpia: 66.
Basilicas, Christian: 8.
BATHS: 96-101.
— of Agrippa: 6, 96.
— of Caracalla: 8, 38, 96-100.
— of Commodus: 96.
— of Constantine: 8.
— of Diocletian: 8, 96, 100-101.
— of Domitian: 96.
— of Nero (Alexandrine): 8, 96.
— of Neptune at Ostia: 116.
— of Septimius Severus: 12.
— of Titus: 67, 96.
— of Trajan: 6, 96.
Bridges:
— of Agrippa: 95.
— of Nero: 95, 105.
— Pons Aelius: 6, 95, 105.
— Pons Aemilius: 94.
— Pons Aurelius: 95.
— Pons Cestius: 94.
— Pons Fabricius: 94.
— Pons Sublicius: 94.
— Ponte Milvio: 95.
Building techniques:
— brickwork: 8, 41-42.
— cement work: 8, 41, 90.
— mixed work: 8.
— reticulated work: 8.
— square work: 8, 77-78.
— uncertain work: 8.

CAMPIDOGLIO: 5, 6, 13, 17, 20, 30-36, 109.
Campus Martius: 5, 6, 8, 32, 37, 55, 90, 95.
Canopus of Hadrian's Villa: 120-121.
Capitolium of Ostia: 116.
Castel Sant'Angelo: 104-105.

Castrum Praetorium: 106.
CATACOMBS: 125-126.
— of Domitilla: 125-126.
— of San Sebastiano: 125.
CIRCUSES: 81-87.
— of Caligula and Nero: 43, 87.
— Flaminius: 81.
— of Maxentius: 43, 86-87, 113.
— Maximus: 10, 12, 43, 44, 81-85.
Clivus Capitolinus: 20, 32.
Cloaca Maxima: 13.
Coelian Hill: 5, 69-70, 109.
COLOSSEUM: 6, 67-79.
Colossus of Augustus: 60.
— of Nero: 67.
Columbaria (sepulchres): 113.
COLUMNS, HONORARY: 22-27, 53-55.
Column of Antoninus Pius: 55.
— of the Decennia: 16.
— of Marcus Aurelius: 55.
— of Phocas: 16.
— of Trajan: 53-54, 66, 123.
Comitium: 13, 16.
Curia: 13, 16, 17, 56.

DOMUS AUREA: 52.
— Augustana: 10, 11.
— Flavia: 11.
— Severiana: 8, 10-11.
— Tiberiana: 10.

Emporium: 95.
Equestrian statue of Domitian: 29.
— of Marcus Aurelius: 32-33.
— of Trajan: 65-66.
Esquiline: 5, 13, 43, 103.

Fasti consolari: 29.
FORUMS, IMPERIAL: 6-8, 56-66.
Forum of Augustus: 6, 56-63.
— Boarium: 5, 37, 95.
— of Caesar: 6, 8, 56-60.
— of the Corporations: 115, 116, 118.
— of Nerva ("Transitory"): 6, 62-64.
— Olitorium: 95.
— of Peace: 6, 38, 62.
FORUM ROMANUM: 5, 6, 13-29, 56.
— of Trajan: 63, 65-66.
Fountain of Juturna: 20.

GARDENS AND VILLAS: 51.
Gardens of Acilii: 106.
— of Sallust: 43.
Gates: see Porta Appia, etc.
Germalus: 9.

HADRIAN'S VILLA, TIVOLI: 44, 119-122.
House of Livia: 10.
— of the Vestals: 21, 26.

Janiculum: 37, 110.

Lapis Niger: 17, 29, 56.
Lateran: 15, 16, 32.
LIBRARIES AND SCHOOLS: 44-45.
Libraries of Augustus: 10.
— of Trajan: 53-54, 66.

Markets of Trajan: 6, 66.
Mausoleums, Imperial: 102-105.
Mausoleum of Augustus: 6, 43, 102-103.
— of Hadrian: 6, 104-105.
— of Romulus son of Maxentius: 113.
Meta Sudans: 67, 110.
Miliarium Aureum: 29.
Mithraea: 37, 100.
Monumentum Ancyranum: 103.
Museums:
— Capitoline: 29, 32-36.
— British: 98.
— of Foligno: 85.
— National of Naples: 98.
— Roman National: 98.
— Vatican: 85, 98-100.

Naumachiae: 95.
Naval dockyards: 95.

OBELISKS: 42-43.
Odeon of Domitian: 6, 90.
OSTIA: 114-118.

PALATINE: 5, 6, 8, 9-12, 13, 16, 24-25, 37, 110.
Palace of Caligula: 10, 16, 24.
PANTHEON: 8, 38, 40-42, 128.
Pincio: 43.
Port of Claudius: 115.
— of Trajan: 115.
Porta Appia (San Sebastiano): 107, 108.
— Aurelia: 108.
— Asinaria: 107.
— Capena: 5.
— Collina: 5, 27.
— Flaminia: 106.
— Fontinalis: 5.
— Latina: 108.
— Metrovia: 108.
— Ostiense (San Paolo): 108.
— Pinciana: 106.
— Portuense: 108.
— Prenestina (Maggiore): 106, 111.
— Salaria: 106.
— Settimiana: 108.
— Tiburtina: 106.
Portico, Aemilian: 8.
— of the Dii Consentes: 17.
— of the Hundred Columns: 6, 90.
— of Octavia: 6.
— of Saepta Julia: 6.
— of Vipsania: 6.
Pyramid of Gaius Cestius: 106, 108.

Quirinal: 5, 8, 43, 62, 63, 103, 109.

Regia: 24.
Res gestae Divi Augusti: 103.
Residential dwellings: 8, 114-115.
ROADS AND COMMUNICATIONS: 112.
Rostra: 13, 16, 56.
— Nova: 27.

Sacellum (Chapel) of Venus Cloacina: 29.
Sanctuary of the Oriental Divinities: 37.
Septizonium: 8, 12, 110.

She-Wolf (Capitoline): 34, 36.
Stadium of Domitian: 6, 88-89.
— Palatine: 11-12.
Sun-dial: 43.
Synagogue of Ostia: 116-117.

Tabularium: 6, 17, 32.
TEMPLES AND RELIGION: 37-39.
Temple of Aesculapius: 94-95.
— of Antoninus and Faustina: 8, 16, 17.
— of Apollo Palatinus: 6, 10.
— of Caesar: 16, 20, 24, 27.
— of Ceres at Ostia: 116, 118.
— of Claudius: 6.
— of the Dioscuri (Castor and Pollux): 16, 17, 20-21, 24.
— of Fortuna Virilis: 37.
— in Forum Boarium (round temple): 37, 38.
— of Hadrian: 8.
— of Isis (Iseo Campense): 37, 43.
— of Janus: 29.
— of Juno Moneta: 30-31, 34.
— of Jupiter Capitolinus: 20, 30, 31, 37.
— of the Magna Mater: 37.
— of Mars Ultor: 6, 60-61, 63.
— of Minerva: 6, 63.
— of Peace: 38.
— of Saturn: 17, 20.
— of Trajan: 53, 66.
— of Venus Genetrix: 6, 56-57.
— of Venus and Rome: 6, 29, 67.
— of Venus at Hadrian's Villa: 122.
— of Vespasian: 17.
— of Vesta: 8, 20-27, 38.
Theatre of Balbus: 90, 92.
— of Marcellus: 90-93, 95.
— of Ostia: 115-118.
— of Pompey: 6, 90, 92.
THEATRES: 90-93.
TIBER: 5, 30, 94-95, 109.
Tiberine Island: 5, 6, 94-95.
Tomb of Cecilia Metella: 113.
— of Geta: 113.
— of the Scipiones: 113.
— of Romulus of Maxentius: 87, 113.
Trastevere: 5.
Trophies of Marius: 111.

Umbilicus Urbis: 29.
URBAN DEVELOPMENT: 5-8.
Ustrinum Antoninorum: 55.

Velia: 9.
VIA APPIA: 5, 112-113.
— dell'Argileto: 62.
— Nova: 25.
— Sacra: 16, 21.
— Tiburtina: 5, 78.
Vicus Longus: 27.
— Tuscus: 21.
— Vestae: 26, 27.

WALLS, AURELIAN: 8, 80, 106-108.
— Republican: 5, 8.
WORKING WORLD: 123-124.

SELECT BIBLIOGRAPHY

Vitruvio, *De Architectura.*
H. Jordan, *Topographie der Stadt Rom im Alterthum.* I, 1 e 2, II. Berlino, 1878, 1885, 1871; I, 3 di C. Hülsen, 1907.
R. Lanciani, *Le Acque e gli Acquedotti di Roma Antica.* Roma, 1881.
T. Mommsen, *Römisches Staatsrecht.* Leipzig, 1887.
R. Lanciani, *The Ruins and Excavations of Ancient Rome.* Londra, 1897.
F. Colagrossi, *L'Anfiteatro Flavio nei suoi venti secoli di storia.* Firenze, 1913.
G. Lugli, *Ville e giardini di Roma Antica.* Roma, 1910.
G. Giovannoni, *La tecnica della costruzione presso i Romani.* Roma, 1925.
G. Gozzo, *Ingegneria Romana.* Roma, 1928.
A. Munoz-A. M. Collini, *Campidoglio.* Roma, 1930.
G. Lugli, *I monumenti antichi di Roma e suburbio,* I-III, « Supplemento ». Roma, 1931-1940.
G. Massano, *Il turismo nell'Antica Roma.* Roma, 1933.
P. Ducati, *L'arte a Roma dalle origini al secolo VIII.* Bologna, 1938.
G. De Angelis D'Ossat, *Tecnica costruttiva e impianti delle terme.* Roma, 1943.
P. Grimal, *Les jardins romains.* Parigi, 1943.
F. G. Lo Bianco, *Storia dei collegi artigiani dell'Impero.* Bologna, 1943.
G. Lugli, *Roma Antica. Il centro monumentale.* Roma, 1946.
G. Moretti, *Ara Pacis Augustae.* Roma, 1948.
L. Homo, *Rome impériale et l'urbanisme dans l'antiquité.* Parigi, 1951.
L. Pareti, *Storia di Roma e del mondo romano.* Torino, 1952.
G. Calza e AA. VV., *Scavi di Ostia.* Roma, 1953.
F. Castagnoli, *Topografia e urbanistica di Roma antica* (ristampa, con correzioni e aggiunte, della prima parte del vol. *Topografia e urbanistica di Roma*). Bologna, 1958.
R. Vighi, *Villa Hadriana.* Roma, 1958.
G. Brand-L. B. Dal Maso, *Hadrian's Villa at Tivoli.* Roma, 1959.
L. Crema, « L'architettura romana », vol. XII dell'*Enc. Class.,* Sez. III. Torino, 1959.
P. Testini, *Le Catacombe e gli antichi cimiteri cristiani in Roma.* Bologna, 1966.
L. Cozzi, *Le porte di Roma.* Roma, 1968.
P. Romanelli, *Il Foro Romano.* Bologna, 1970.
G. Baracconi, *Spettacoli nell'antica Roma.* Roma, 1972.
J. B. Ward-Perkins, *Architettura romana.* Venezia, 1974.
L. B. Dal Maso - R. Vighi, *Ostia - Porto - Isola Sacra.* Firenze, 1975.
L. B. Dal Maso - R. Vighi, *Tivoli - Villa Adriana - Subiaco - Valle dell'Aniene.* Firenze, 1975.
J. Carcopino, *La vita quotidiana a Roma.* Traduz. it. Bari, 1976.
U. E. Paoli, *Vita romana.* Vicenza, 1976.